MW01167135

The Occasion of Man

God's Invited Guests and Relatives

—⁓—

L. Smith
(256) 694-9704

MICHAEL DAWSON SR., M.B.A.

To
Cheryl Sapp
God Bless You and Your
Family Aug 30, 2003

Content

—⁓—

Forward

—ᴠᴠ—

The Occasion of Man — God's Invited Guests and Relatives — is a solid and diverting book that can be read by anyone who has a serious desire of developing a solid Biblical foundation about God's purposes in sending His Son Jesus Christ into this world to save man from his sins. It is a thought-provoking book and gives some powerful nuggets that can inspire any reader to better daily living.

Michael Dawson begins the book with an interesting story about "Take down the sign" and from that point the book takes the reader on a journey with a series of stops that ultimately ends where he started with Jesus and Christ, and His purpose for coming into the world — to save man from sin.

Dawson is not a novice to solid Biblical theological discussion. He starts with the first chapter with Abraham the Son of Promise and ends in chapter nine with a Call to Commitment in Jesus Christ, and sandwiched in between is the exploration of some very deep thoughts that even the most unlearned can grasp and plumb.

I recommend this book for inclusion of any serious Bible student in their personal library.

Randolph Bracy, Jr., M.Div, Ed.D.

Preface

—ᴍ—

E ach author has a specific purpose and goal in mind when deciding to embark upon such a task as writing a book. Therefore, it is fitting to give you this author's passion for writing the "Occasion". This book is written with the new Christian in mind, in an effort to improve quality of life. It introduces to the reader information necessary to simplify some of the controversial mystic pertaining to our Christian background. In Robert Herrick, Counsel To Girls, young girls are admonished to make the highest and best use of their prime. This book holds that same urgency for the newly saved Christian, because they are at the most critical point in life. They are at the point where reading the Bible may not be a way of life, it may even seem hard, strange, or foreign to them.

The Occasion foundation is based on solid Biblical truths. In chapter 1 The Provisional Promise features events from the life and times of Abraham. Chapters 2 define and discuss deception with regards to Old and New Testament standards. Chapter 3 gives you a quick peek into the though process behind Paul's letter to the Ephesians. Chapter 4 is all about deliverance and salva-tion. Chapter 5 clarifies our need to communicate with our eternal creator via prayer. Chapter 6 introduces the mysteries of God. Chapter 7 one of the most important chapters in this book lays out forgiveness and discusses our reason for needing to forgive. Chapter 8 let you look back over your shoulder and see the coming of Jesus. This bring us to the end of the book Chapter 9 calling for us to become students and followers of Jesus, then the reference

God's Invited Guests and Relatives

—◊◊◊—

What do you do when you are expecting family members or visitors to come to your home for vacation, lunch, or just to sit and talk awhile? Most people including myself generally roll out the red carpet, so to speak. We make everything as close to perfect as possible. The floor must be freshly cleaned; presentation of the living area must be pleasing to the eye, and food of sorts in place. Well, before creation, God does the same for His specially Invited guests. He made everything and inspected each item, then pronounces it as being good. When all of creation is perfect, God extended the invitation to man. Then from the dust of the earth God transforms us into royalty making our entry into the world bold and with ultimate supremacy over all creation. We were created in the image of God, sinless creatures with only the nature of love. Later the word is out that man has fallen from grace and we need a savior. We need Jesus. But when He does come to the creation made by His own hands, we did not extend that same welcome to Him. We gave Him the worst of the worst. Now the occasion of man redefines itself to the task of preaching the gospel to everyone willing to listen. God loves you, so preach it and give someone else the same opportunity that God gives to you.

INTRODUCTION

Introduction

—⁂—

E very event has a prompt that cause an occasion to happen, and that something is the "But For" or reason for the occasion. Consider this, Jesus came into the world as the means of salvation for all people, "But For," no other reason than to redeem us from the "Sins" of our forefather Adam. Therefore, in syllogistically chronology the occasion was Jesus' visit, the cause of his visit was to save us from sin and the results of His coming is our salvation. In most cases the occasion depends on other intermediate objectives for its success. That is, once the occasion is determined, before and during the event, other supporting activities must be in place to further the event.

It was not enough that Jesus despised sin and wanted us free from it; He had to put in place the right people and teach them how to service the event. Jesus knew that his mission was the healing and redemption of the world, and that He was the only sacrifice good enough to go on the bonds for humankind. However, every occasion must start somewhere. We must have a point in which we can look upon as being the beginning. We as Christians have the Bible therefore we need not guess or speculate about our beginning because it is all spelled out. God tells us in his Word where the beginning or starting point is in the book of Genesis.

Genesis is the first book of the Bible, it tells the story of creation (Gen. 1 and 2). As the definition has it, Genesis means the beginning or origin. The book of Genesis does more than just tell the story of our beginning, it is the foundation on which all other books of the Bible rests, and it provides a historical picture of how the enemy (Satan) hates God and wants to separate us (humans) from God. Jesus said that a wise person will build his house on a solid foundation (Matt 7:24) so that it will be able to stand during turbulent times. Therefore, God has given us the Bible and the Prophets or men of God in support of His primary objective. He has given us the Bible as the foundation of our belief system, to let us have a glimpse of the past, and Prophets or men of God gaze at tomorrow and show us the otherwise unknown future. We are blessed to have such a God who cares for us and to reflect the commentary of our lives in the pages of His book, the Bible.

Jesus gave a brief analysis of the Bible; He looked at Genesis as being the starting point or foundation and structure on which all else is constructed and supported. Genesis is the foundation and the rest of the Bible is the superstructure. The superstructure or building above ground shows the rendering of our lives from Genesis until this very day. Therefore, we can conclude that God has given us a solid foundation on which we can build. We must stand on the word of God and not every wind of doctrine (Eph. 4:14). If we do not follow the guidance of the Bible, then the fault of our calamities lie at our own door steps. We as men and women of God are not just responsible for our own actions and well being, we are to admonish and give wise counsel to all brothering that none be lost. In essence, we are to enable and strengthen the brother or sister of a lower degree to a solid place in the Lord. We must include everyone as a full member and partner of the unified body of Christ.

Consider the books of Matthew, Mark, Luke, and John as cameras that bring into focus the occasion of a discernible majestic man who was sent to earth by the almighty God. These images bring into focus the Lion, Man, the Ox and the Eagle to render the great revelations of their message. Matthew, Mark, and Luke are in synoptic parallelism, whereas John's compatibility is different. Matthew is a Lion, showing Jesus as the Messiah "The Lion of Judah." Mark is the man; his message is the most down to earth, straightforward and human of all the gospels. Luke is the Ox; he saw Jesus as the great servant and final sacrifice. John is the Eagle because the eagle is the only bird that can fly looking directly at the sun and maintain clear vision. John's gospel gives us the most penetrating gaze into the eternal mysteries of Jesus **(DBS William Barclay, P1, 1975, 2nd ED)**. Collectively their mission was simply to tell the good news of Jesus and salvation to everyone willing to listen. The occasion, Jesus Christ, is the compelling news and salvation is the message that lifts our hopes high toward heaven on the sheer wings of faith. Salvation through Jesus Christ is our most precious gift from the heart of God to the soul of man. Jesus comes to us for one defining purpose predestined from the beginning of the world; His death, burial and resurrection **(Romans 6:3–12)**. Through Jesus, God has already done everything necessary to complete my message; now all I have to do is spill the beans **(Mark 16:15–18)**.

Salvation

Looking at my testimony and what God is saying to people through me; simply put, my message is salvation. Jesus is the occasion, the core reality of our needs, and the reason for our salvation. Today we as a whole are operating as though salvation is dated and no longer matters **(Pastor William Abernathy)**. We have that business as usual mentality; we are opened on Sundays and closed for the rest of the week. What if God operated in the same manner? God wants more from us than that; He wants our hearts always OPENED so that we may declare His good news. Consider this short example: During my tenure in the military one of my assignments was Fort Riley, "Home of the Big Red One." Upon receiving orders, my family and I packed the car and we headed for Kansas. After driving for a while it soon becomes night and the vehicle is low on fuel. Everyone in the car was asleep with the exception of Kesha "my co-driver (human GPS)." Her job was to read the map and navigate the vehicle, however, now the vehicle is almost empty and no gas stations are in sight; concerns ran high. Later down the freeway, we see a sign saying gas ahead. We follow the sign for about two miles down some dark road to a gas station. When we arrive at the station, it is lifeless. Later one of the residents tells us that the store has been closed for almost five years. We turned around and headed back to the freeway. Then Kesha says, "If they had gone out of business, why did they not take down the sign"?

Conclusion

My message and the message in this book is to everyone, from the standard pew sitter on seat no# 77, deacons, ministers, pastors, and churches as a whole is this. God wants people to know and preach salvation, because salvation is serious, and if you have gone out of business, then take down the sign **(Kesha M. Dawson).** Some think of the preaching and teaching ministry solely as an opportunity for status, notoriety, a profession, or job **(Pastor Richard King).** However, I see it differently; it is our opportunity to deliver the good news about salvation in and through the Lord and Savior Jesus Christ. Because I take my salvation and the salvation of others seriously, I am forever careful when witnessing to anyone. With me, the sign over my heart will always say "opened" to defend and speak on the occasion and goodness of Jesus, because like Abraham, I am the promised seed.

CHAPTER 1

—⁓—

The Provisional Promise

—ⱳ—

Looking back at the life of Abraham, we see a man with common frailties like unto any other human. Still we have made him our hero, that perfect man. This is a perilous thing because at some point in time, your hero will let you down. Consider Jimmy Swaggart, Richard M. Nixon, Bill Clinton, Jim Baker and others that people have elevated above life to hero status; they all let the people down. However, there is one that sticks closer to you than a brother; He will never let you down, and is forever faithful. His name is Jesus. Now Abraham had a few bouts of his own; God tells him to leave his family and go to a land that I will show you, but he takes Lot with him, and then he was mendacious about his relationship to Sarah. However, when we study the story of Abraham, we learn that it's not about Abraham the man. It is a portrait of our relationship, and how we should trust in God.

Abraham was an able role model and is used as an example of how far God would go to keep His promises to us. Once God makes a promise, it must be fulfilled. God told Abraham that his seed would be as the sand on beach and stars in the heaven, and that "all the nations shall be blessed through him." Sarah must also be included as an active part of this picture for promises to unfold. God does not separate the family, He bonds them closer together. Therefore, Sarah must give Abraham a son; otherwise the property or inheritance would go to the elder servant of the house. The result is the end of Abraham's blood line, in short "no promises." However, Abraham believed God and God counted it to him for righteousness; thus the promise is fulfilled.

Throughout the Bible God tells us of His plan for our redemption. He has made us the seed of Abraham, and we, if we believe in His son Jesus, it shall be counted to us for righteous. Now that we have talked about the promise, where and how does it all start?

Phase I Background Genesis 6–25

Genesis Chapter (3) three marks the climax of a one sided world. Prior to Genesis (3) all in the earth was only good. God said so, and blessed everything including the Sabbath day. Then lured by Satan, dealing from the bottom of the deck, Eve and Adam were coached into making the wrong choice. As a result of Adam disobeying God to achieve self-deification, we have lost that loving feeling of oneness with our creator and now it's gone – gone - gone. That child like dependence would vanish forever and man would continue to worsen. Over a period of just six (6) chapters man's condition deteriorates and the evilness in man's spirit robs God of His glory, therefore in our natural condition we are at constant enmity with God and cannot please Him (Roman 8:7). So God cleans up the earth and starts afresh.

In this fresh start, God brings us to a microscopic mustard seed point in history that seemed insignificant to everybody except one man (Abraham.) Even though Abraham and the household he lived in worshipped false gods, and made enchantments, God chose him. God made far reaching promises to Abraham, which would enable us to survive the curse brought on by Adam. Our survival is brought through Abraham via the person of Jesus Christ. Now at this juncture you may wonder why God would play with us for over 2000 years, instead of just issuing the Great Commission. For this question I do not have an answer, but I do know that Jesus came at the fullness of time and brought forth the final redemption for mankind. Then if our final redemption came on the heels of promises God made to Abraham, what was the promises, under what condition could we receive the promises, and could the benefits of these promises be transferred to Abraham's heirs. The answer to these questions exposits to Noah from the end of the flood in Genesis chapter 8, and continues to our rest in Jesus.

The end of the flood (Gen 8:20–9:29)

Now that the flood is all over, it is time for the damage assessment, and after action activities to take place. Just as God has taken care of Noah, his family and all that were with him through the storms. He also does the same for us. When the storms of life come in hard after us and we are shut in for forty days and nights, it may seem that the end will never come. But, behind every dark cloud there is a silver lining, so just keep the faith and nothing wavering. God Himself will bring you out of your tribulations, and set you off to a new beginning. In Hebrews 13:5 God says that He will never leave or forsake you. Even after the end of the storms, it is not uncommon for us to feel forsaken. The feeling of abandonment is a natural human emotion. The children of Israel felt forsaken and abandoned by Moses, Paul said in 2nd Corinthians that because of his troubles in Asia, he almost gave up on life, in Matthews 27:46 Jesus dying on the cross felt the separation and abandonment from God and cries out "My God, My God, why hast thou forsaken me? Therefore, feeling cast out is not a new emotion. God has not forgotten, but remembers us.

Here in Genesis 8:1 Noah and all that are with him are remembered. This does not mean in any way that God had at any point forgotten them. Because it is impossible for God to forget anything, He knows everything from the ending to the beginning and visa versa. Relatively, it means that God has fulfilled His promise on behalf of Noah. For it is the characteristic of an immutable God that's perfect in every way not to change; we can trust in His assurance. Even though Noah believed and trusted God, it was not enough because God looks at the family. It's a family matter, his wife, sons, and daughters in law must also exemplify that same faith in God's assurance. Now that God has fulfilled His promises and trouble is behind them, it is time to start anew. So God rewards Noah and his family for their faith and told them to be fruitful and multiply, and multiply they did. However, before all the multiplying got under way, a few bumps and obstacles appear in the road.

Noah's sacrifice to God and God's covenant with the Earth. (Gen 8:2–9;19)

Noah was so glad to get off the Ark onto dry land. His first order of business was to build an Alter to make sacrifices unto God. The Bible does not tell what kind of sacrifice it was, neither does it matter, as long as it sent out a sweet smell savor unto the Lord. The phrase, sweet smelling savor is descriptive of Gods level of satisfaction and acceptance of the sacrifice. The impact of God's acceptance wraps our salvation in a nice neat package. Noah and his family was saved from the storm by the Ark and we are saved from the storm of sin by the beloved son of God, in the resurrection of Jesus Christ (Matt 12:38–40). After the flood, God not only made a covenant not to destroy the earth again, but blessed Noah with the bounty of the land. He became a Husbandman. A husbandman is more than just a farmer, he is in companionship with the land itself. His children were blessed as well.

Noah's Prophecy concerning the future of his children:

Every new beginning starts somewhere, and as with Noah he is the roots or foundation that supports the annals of history. This family legacy typifies the tables of repopulation and the future of mankind. It is here where Canaan is cursed and others are blessed. Abraham is from the blessed of the blessed seed.

Phase II Abraham zeitgeist (Genesis 11:27–20:18)

Family history

If we look at the past in regards to Abraham and review the written records concerning his life and the generation following him, we see the promises of God fulfilled. The Bible shows in systematic analysis and continuous narrative of how God prepared the heart of one man to be the father and leader of our nation. His footsteps were ordered by the Lord and vicariously I shall let you walk a mile in them. We shall follow this man who God called "Friend" because he stands out bigger than life in both the Old and New Testament. This man did not hesitate to move forward in faith after receiving the call from God. We as the church must do likewise. Consider the character of Abraham and ask yourself, why God needs such a person as Abraham. Well the answer is laid out between the pages of Genesis chapter 1–11. Chapter 1–11 is by comparison what a foundation is to a building, the frame or chasse is to an automobile, or ethic is to law. It is the backbone on which the rest of the Bible rests.

Let's go on that 2000 year old trip and stop in at some of the sites. Chapters 1–2 the creation, Chapter 3 is the fall of man and the origin of sin, Chapter 4 the first murder, Chapters 6–9 wickedness grows and God prosecutes the sins of society. Even with all this evil, man is given another chance through Noah. God rose up a new order of man, but the heart of man has not changed. Therefore, man has failed again; but, because of God's love for mankind he zeros in on Abraham and sets him apart as the beginning of the redemptive process. Abraham did not know or choose God, God chose him and the journey begins.

a. Mission to leave Ur (11:27–32)

At this point in time we see Terra, Abraham's father is in control of the family and takes on the mission to go to Canaan, but like Gilligan, he became shipwrecked and began to enjoy the comforts of the island. He stops short on his journey in a city called Haran. Haran is that trick of the enemy that seems to offer all of the connivances for prosperity and the good life. Therefore Terra stayed there until His death. Unlike Terra, we as Christians do not have to stop short of our salvation, because Jesus has already made the journey for us. The death of Terra still leaves his household intact, therefore Abraham must leave.

b. Mission to leave Haran

Although Abraham is 75 years old, this kind of mission is something new to him, but like his forefather Enoch, and Noah, he had the faith to believe in the divine power of God.

Terra is now dead, and the Lord says unto Abraham, "It is time to make the decision whether or not you will remain of the household of your father Terra, or break free to establish your own." God focuses in on Abraham and calls him to independence telling him it is time to move away from everything he knows; his country, his kindred, and from his father's house and go unto a land that I will show you. This action may at our stage in grace seem like baby steps in comparison to the finished work of deliverance. However, these baby steps toddle deep into our emancipation because

God has decided to cover our sins through one man. One man in spite of his present condition as a worshipper of false gods and a worshipper of idols will foster the channel whereby our savior will come into the world.

Contrasting the mentality of humans to the love of God, some of us would have probably cut Abraham out of the picture altogether and sent Jesus to die for the sins of man as early as Gen 12: We would have taken that "Just do it" attitude of Nike and activated the Great Commission. This is not the ways of God, and like it or not, He is not bound to follow our script.

Abraham like many Christians in the beginning almost obeys God. He makes the move from Haran, but brings the past with him. God commanded him to leave it all behind, but he brought Lot with him. When we bring baggage from the past along our Christian journey, it will cause the same kind of problems in our lives now as it did before we were saved. After we confess Christ and say that we are a Christian, there are just some things that we should leave behind. Things like, going to the night clubs to party, drinking alcohol or using drugs, sleeping around, or even viewing xxx rated movies. The corresponding problems caused by these strongholds will not diminish just because we say we are a Christian. You must be obedient to God and leave them behind. However, the portraits of both Terra and Lot do show clearly the pictures of what not to do in our relationship with the Father.

Terra is the representation of the person who intends to give his/her life to Christ but keep falling short as the rich young ruler did. He comes to church, accepts the invitation of the pastor to come down front, goes to another part of the church and Sister Barbara, and the prayer team pray with him/her, but never gives his/her life to Christ. Whereas, Lot says that he accepts Christ, but soon returns to a backslidden condition because his commitment was only temporary. Commitment and not double minded (James 1:6) is a characteristic that Christians must possess. Jesus says (Matt 6:24) you cannot serve two masters. Therefore, the journey to Canaan may sometimes be tuff and test our loyalty, but God is able to take us through the test so that we may claim our inheritance (Phil 1:6). So, therefore, what are the promises of the covenant, terms and conditions, and are they transferable.

God's Covenant to Abraham (Gen 12:1–4 & 15:1–5)

Genesis 12:1-3 (KJV) [1] Now the LORD had said unto Abram, Get thee out of thy country, and from thy kindred, and from thy father's house, unto a land that I will shew thee: [2] And I will make of thee a great nation, and I will bless thee, and make thy name great; and thou shalt be a blessing: [3] And I will bless them that bless thee, and curse him that curseth thee: and in thee shall all families of the earth be blessed.

Genesis 15:1-6 (KJV) [1] After these things the Word of the LORD came unto Abram in a vision, saying, Fear not, Abram: I am thy shield, and thy exceeding great reward. [2] And Abram said, Lord GOD, what wilt thou give me, seeing I go childless, and the steward of my house is this Eliezer of Damascus? [3] And Abram said, Behold, to me thou hast given no seed: and, lo, one born in my house is mine heir. [4] And, behold, the Word of the LORD came unto him, saying, "This shall not be thine heir; but he that shall come forth out of thine own bowels shall be thine heir."
[5] And he brought him forth abroad, and said, "Look now toward heaven and tell the stars if thou be able to number them: and he said unto him, So shall thy seed be." [6] And he believed in the LORD; and he counted it to him for righteousness.
Before we can answer the question, about the covenant between God and Abraham, we must first set the boundaries

in describing a covenant. The covenant as made in Gen 12:3 is without conditions just obedience. The agreement between the two parties God and Abraham lack the elements of our basic contracts. Abraham did not have to give up anything of value, put anything in writing using formal terms and if he was not able to live up to the agreement God makes Himself responsible for the breach. Therefore, Abraham's half of the contract was only childlike obedience. The promises in the covenant to Abraham were (1) Gen. 12:1 Abraham is promised to be a great nation (land), (2) Gen. 15:4 that his own son shall be his heir, and (3) Gen. 12:2 he would be a blessing to all nations. Counting the blessing one by one let's take a look at the first blessing; it is of abundance and increase (great nation and land). God tells Abraham to Gen. 15:5 (KJV) Look now toward heaven, and tell the stars, if thou be able to number them: and he said unto him, So shall thy seed be. (a) Gen. 15:18 (KJV)[18] In the same day the LORD made a covenant with Abram, saying, Unto thy seed have I given this land, from the river of Egypt unto the great river, the river Euphrates: this is the picture of abundance. (b)God is giving Abraham more than enough, but why does Abraham need all of that property, could he just share the space with another country already established. The answer is a qualified "NO." The factors that qualify "NO:"(1) As long as Abraham's descendents are in another country, they are under the authority of man; God wants them for His people. (2) it does not matter how many members are added to their census (as in Egypt) they would amount to no more than a large ethnic group; God wants them to be a nation. Gen 15:4 that his own son shall be his heir. The key scripture text in this segment (Gen. 15:6) elevate the blessing beyond that of the land and wealth, it does something personal for Abraham himself. It justifies him, and justification incorporates to total summation of God's benefits (Rom 4:1–25). Abraham is justified because of faith and not works and is forgiven of all his sins forever. Genesis 22 specifies conditions for the promises, Therefore, are they obtained by works? Here again the answer is a qualified "NO." No because works and obedience are not the same. Works says Bernard Burrell in his narrative (philosophy of the body), is what the body must do in order to maintain and sustain its reciprocal interaction, but the obedience Abraham had was from his faith in God. This does not mean that Abraham becomes non-caporal living as an angel and will never sin again, because he does. But now that Abraham is justified by God, God has written this covenant to pardon our sins. (3) Gen 12:2 he would be a blessing to all nations. Abraham is to be the means whereby all people that believe in Christ shall be saved. His name means Father of many nations not just to the Jewish community of people. The names given to children illustrated the family closeness to God, the syllable ab means father (These Were God's People, William C. Martin, M. A., B. D., 1966, p27)

Terms and conditions of the covenant

When we look at a general contract between humans, we must consider every angle of agreement before signing. If the conditions are not acceptable then our first step in establishing a meeting of the minds is to negotiate the objectionable parts. If both parties agree with the language, it is made legal by signing. The signing means that we agree with the outcome elicited by a specifiable incentive. A covenant of this nature is not 100% solid because it depends on both parties upholding their end of the bargain. Now let's look at the substance of the covenant between God and Abraham. In Gen 12:1-5 and Gen 15:4-5 there is no indication of any conditions on the part of Abraham. Genesis 15:9 –17 describes the ritual of cutting a covenant. When a covenant during the days of Abraham is cut between two people it involves a binding process whereby an animal is sacrificed. The animal is divided into halves and placed on opposite sides of each other on the ground. The two parties seal the deceleration to keep their promise by walking between the pieces. Meaning that if they fail to keep the agreement, may the same thing happen to them as to this animal. However, the event between God and Abraham was different in that only God alone passes between the pieces. Showing the one-sided solemnizing of unconditional grace. So there is no way the agreement can fail. However, in Gen 22:16-18 we find there are conditions, for in Genesis 22:15-18 (KJV) the angel of the LORD called unto Abraham out of heaven the second time, [16] And said, By myself have I sworn, saith the LORD, for because thou hast done this thing, and hast not withheld thy son, thine only son: [17] That in blessing I will bless thee, and in multiplying I will multiply thy seed as the stars of the heaven, and as the sand which is upon the sea shore; and thy seed shall possess the gate of his enemies; [18] And in thy seed shall all the nations of the earth be blessed; because thou hast obeyed my voice.

Based on this language, it would seem that the redemption of man rested squarely on the success of Abraham. But in accordance with Ezekiel 36:27 (KJV) [27] God says, And I will put my spirit within you, and cause you to walk in my statutes, and ye shall keep my judgments, and do them. The meaning is that God has equipped Abraham not to fail; therefore the covenant is both conditional and secure.

Heirs to the Covenant.

Now that we have determined that the covenant between God and Abraham will happen, and that Abraham will continue to live as a human; then like other humans; at some point he must join the great people who sleep in the earth. Because this is inevitable, God has made it so that the benefits of his covenant would pass onto heirs. In Genesis 17:4 the unfolding of the promise is simplified 4"As for me, behold, my covenant is with thee, and thou shalt be a father of many nations." Paul says in Romans 9:6–8) that the umbrella of Abraham will cover more than just the Jewish nation it is for us all, and that not all of Israel is of Israel. Meaning that, the individual who gives his/her life to Christ will inherit the promises, and if someone of the seed of Abraham does not accept Christ, then they shall be lost. In retrospect, consider this: salvation is to Isaac and not Ishmael, Jacob and not Esau as being in line for the fullness of God's promises. The promises of God shall not fail and we shall inherit everlasting life through Jesus Christ.

How can we be certain that our inheritance is secure and that Abraham lived up to his end of the bargain? Near the end of his life, Abraham (Gen. 24:1–9) calls his chief servant and sends him on a mission to get a wife for Isaac from his own people. He makes his servant swear in the Name of the Lord. God leads the servant directly to Rebekah and prospers his way. The servant's testimony about Abraham is a lifetime of faithfulness with the Lord (Gen. 24:27) saying blessed be the Lord, the God of my master Abraham, who has not forsaken his steadfast love and faithfulness toward my master. Abraham being justified benefits from the full promises of God, and we being the seed of Abraham will inherit. Because God tell us in Exodus 3:15 "I am the God of Abraham" meaning that the eternal creator is our God and nothing can destroy that relationship. Satan makes a last ditch effort to put an end to that relationship by killing Jesus on the Cross, but three days later God raises Jesus from the dead, because Jesus belonged to God. And we the seed of Abraham belong to Jesus, therefore we belong to God, and when God is your God, death can't end the relationship.

CHAPTER 2

Deception

—ᴠᴠ—

During one of our regular Sunday sermons, Bishop Kimble talks about the deceitfulness of man and where it all begins. He goes on to state further that, although the tongue is said to be untamable; before the utterance of any message from the tongue, the beginning of that message has already been formulated within the heart. For whatsoever, man believes and considers in his heart, that will the mouth speak. It is from deep within an individual that determines the type of person they are. Matthew 12:35 (KJV) 35 A good man out of the good treasure of the heart bringeth forth good things: and an evil man out of the evil treasure bringeth forth evil things.

As previously stated, what we ascribe to will ultimately determine not only who we are, but the way we act and think. We can only camouflage the visual boundaries of our physical and spiritual being with colors that match the background of the Christian faith for so long. Then like mama (Bernice Johnson, mother n law) says, at some point the cover will come off to expose the monkey underneath. All of those half-truths carefully concealed between good information must surface. Good information cloaked with lies imbedded in the lives of people can cause them to deceive both themselves and others into thinking that they are something that they are not. A man portraying himself as a woman

35

and vice versa is an example of one of America's massive deceptive movements of the homosexual community. They borrow from the pages of Sherlock Holmes disguise manual, and paint themselves as the opposite sex, put on gay parades to show their pride, and even bring about legislation to obtain national recognition, but the effects of this manipulation is not enough. We can look at the person and relatively see what they are, just as Christians who RAP (Read And Pray) can easily tell when something does not align itself with the word of God. Even more so, deception is an evil game, when we consider the tricks and the end results from the view point of the person or persons being swindled, misinformed or deceived. So what is deception?

What is Deception?

Emily Dickinson writes in her poem of inoculation, "tell the truth but tell it slant," in the world of academia it means that the truth should be total entirely, but without substance and later then when the substance of the truth do appear, the impact will be softer. This type of thinking breeds deception, fraud, unfair dealing, subterfuge, and trickery causing us to worship from an impure heart. Staring closer at Genesis chapter 13–19, Luke 17:28 -33, and 2 Peter 2:6–9 the camera bring into focus true worship and deceptive worship. Lot, the nephew of Abraham is highlighted, his story is told not because he was a sinful person, but because he learned to love and enjoy the benefits of sinful Sodom. Lot was raised and travels in the camp with Abraham, sing the same songs, and acknowledge Abraham's God. On the surface it seems that Lot is a true worshipper of God, but if he is not then why tell his story. The tale of Lot weaves itself in different segments of Abraham's story to show by contrast and comparison the character of Abraham and his relationship to God. Lot joins Abraham at the beginning of his journey and follows him to Canaan because he starts out a true believer. He believed that God promised to bless Abraham to be a great nation and that his seeds would be as the sand on the beaches and the stars in the heavens. Lot was temporally a righteous man as indicated in 2 Peter 2:6-9 (KJV). 2 Peter 2:6-9 spotlights Lot and his family as being the righteous among the wicket. Thus it reads as follows, [6] And turning the cities of Sodom and Gomorrha into ashes condemned them with an overthrow, making them an example unto those that after should live ungodly; [7] And delivered just Lot, vexed with the filthy conversation of the wicked: [8] (For that righteous man dwelling among them, in seeing and hearing, vexed his righteous soul from day to day with their unlawful deeds;) [9] The Lord knoweth how to deliver the godly out of temptations, and to reserve the unjust unto the day of judgment to be punished:

Lot is delivered, but Satan has not given up on him. Satan has the weight of time and cares of the world on his side to deceive Lot into choosing the good times and opportunities in Sodom over his relationship with God. Satan wears us down, as he did Lot by putting things in our lives that move us away from God and closer to Sodom; thing that cause us to fall in love with the world, then he just waits. Lot however was delivered by God, not because he deserved it, but because of God's goodness and mercy. We have the opportunity to look back and see this picture fully develop and repent of our sins. In addition we have the opportunity to come to Christ and cause others to follow us. And because of Christ, our family lines are expanded to include all of the people of the world that Love the Lord and do the will of God. The will of God is for the salvation of mankind through obedience to His son Jesus. Obedience because, Jesus is God's perfect sacrifice for sin; therefore we must not look back at the world and die in Sodom.

The accounts of Lot also tell the story of Jesus Christ who died for everyone, not just for the Abrahams, but the

Lots of the world can be saved as well. Paul writes, where sin abounds, grace does much more abound. Now does that mean, since Jesus has paid the price for us we can do anything we want and still be saved. Well, the answer to this question emerges from the impact of Genesis chapter 11–26 showing that we are saved by Jesus through grace and mercy, but we must live obedient to the word of God. Living obedient to the word of God is not works, because you cannot obtain salvation via your own efforts.

Truth and Half Truths

Often we here people use the phrase, I am telling the truth. Well, what is truth and how does it accommodate our agenda. The truth is narrow in concept but wide in variations. When we look at this simple word "truth," it seems easy enough, but when asked to explain it, simplicity kind of hides in the mist of intellectual combat. We say that truth is a concept of conformity to reality, facts, and what actually happens. Then is this truth or our interpretation of truth as we apply the functions of conformity, facts and reality. Using the proverbs of halves, we say that in order to go to the church we must get at least half way there, and from there half way again and so on until we finally reach the church. But in reality using this table we will never reach that church because of infinity one half. But in reality we can reach the church, and can never reach the church.

When we link ourselves with leadership that will only spoon feed us the truth from fear of not being politically correct the church members will as a whole will never reach the fullness of God's promises. Deception does not just come from the unjust (Col. 2:8) only; it can be preached from the tradition of man rather than the Word of God. Before we can say that something is true, we must validate that the statements made are in fact true (How to Think Straight, Anthony Flew, 2002) by determining if any part of that statement is in fact false. God is all truth, Satan is all error, and truth is not relative to anything other than itself. Relativism (**http:// www.friesian.com/relative.htm**) says that everything is true base on the person's definition of truth. Relativism leads us on a scavenger hunt for what is really true. If we set out to prove that relativism is true or false then, if relativism is true, it must not fail in either case. If I say that relativism is false for me and by relativism my statement is true, then relativism is false (it fails). However, if you say that my statement about relativism is only false for me, and that it is true for you, then relativism fails the truth test in at least one place again, therefore it is false. The conclusion is that truth is not self contradictory. So then what is truth? Jesus said "I am the Truth" meaning that the truth as He was from God and absolute, needing nothing beyond that reality.

Lies

If the earth is some kind of island or resort for the truth, then move over because lies have packed its bags and are co-existing. Moses warned us in the book of Deuteronomy that false prophets, teaching false doctrines, are indeed a threat because some are so believable that if it was possible they would fool the very elect. Off times it is not easy to distinguish the difference between mystifying falsities appealing the human heart than the genuine article. The New Age Religion has released a statement saying that within the span of 20 years (from 1989) most preachers would teach their doctrine, regardless of their religious preference or background. Part of this indoctrination process is to provide free or reduce priced pre-written materials, like ready scripted sermons and commentaries. This is believable because we live in the age of an information society, with thousands of libraries at our finger tips, so what do we use to test the validity of all this information. We lay it on scripture, Paul says that, All Scripture is profitable for teaching, for reproof, for correction, for training in righteousness" (2 Tim. 3:16). Therefore, the wheat and tears can grow together and in the end God will do the separating.

However, on the other side of the picture is the opposing sprit or the spirit of error. Satan first encounter with mankind was one of deception, his primary objective was to lead man in the wrong direction. Today, examples of that same spirit continues, consider this, on (September, 25, 2008) thousands of people depending of a dealership chain owned Bill Herd have been deceived. They were lied to about the conditions of the company until the last day when it closed. The major reason for closing was not the economy, but unethical practices that caused legal activity to surmount against all of his dealerships. ["In July 2007, Bill Heard also faced a $50 million deceptive advertising lawsuit and was bombarded with a litany of complaints from consumers in the states where it operates (**http://www.bizjournals.com/ houston/stories/2008/09/22/daily35.html**)"] in short summation, to Bill Heard Auto dealerships the truth was relative. They were deceivers and counterfeiters, like the false prophets that Moses speaks of in Deuteronomy. Counterfeit items sometimes look and seam to operate as well as the item it is imitating. Counterfeit items, in most cases achieve its purpose. When I was in Korea, the local vender selling brand name shoes and clothing advertises this slogan, "We have the best counterfeit brands in Korea, therefore buy from us." Jesus is not looking for the best counterfeit Christians in the world; he wants the pure 100% sold out person(s). We can achieve that 100% because the Holy Spirit is here to keep our mind on Jesus and to do what's good not evil.

System governing the world

Good and Evil

What is evil, is it the opposite of good, or something more? Shortly, I will attempt to show illustrations of both good and evil situations, and then blend them into meaningful solutions for your consideration. You may not have to go further than the television in your home to find evil lurking around. For example, when we turn on the set and hear of unnecessary human suffering such as a baby left in the car with the windows rolled up, and the temperature above 120F; while the parents go shopping. This kind of torment and inhumane treatment is evil, God wants only good things for our lives, but sometimes those things are skewed to our misfortune. That good thing that God meant for us is now twisted into evil because somehow we have taken Him out of the picture. The word tells us that we will reap the harvest of that we sow, but sometimes evil come upon us without a cause. Consider Job, a righteous man, a man who trust and fear God. The Bible says in the book of Job; that Job was morally straight and shunned evil. Job follows and reverences God with his whole being, he was a unique person, but in just a few short verses, thing would go wrong. The news coming to Job is all evil, and like Job, we may off times wonder; what have I done that merits all this pain. When questions like this come up, just remember how at the end God answers Job with abundantly more than he starts with. God will take the evil and turn it into something good.

God can take the evil that people direct toward you and turn it into good. Joseph was the pampered son of a pampered son Jacob. His eleven brothers, makes him an outcast and then plan evil against him. At first they wanted to just kill him and stop the dreams, then later modified the thinking to something equally as bad; they sold him into slavery. Their evil scheme unfolds in reverse, instead of the dreams stopping, he not only continues to dream, but is giving the gift to interpretations of dreams. The evil they meant to him was counteracted by the blessing God put on his life. God has blessed him to execute on the physical level the promises of Abraham, "Your seed shall be a blessing to all nations." Joseph was able to save himself, his family and the surrounding nations from starvation during the famine.

Now that we have established that there is a difference between good and evil and no indication has been offered to show similarities between the two. It is fitting that we discuss the systems governing the world that we live in; the systems of good and evil exclusively. The system of good is of God, while the system of evil belongs to Satan, and Satan's master plan is to induce disobedience toward God. In Genesis 3:1-24, the disobedience of Adam and Eve seem to come quickly in the Bible, but the results linger. God has given us the Holy Spirit to keep us from getting caught up in a moment of plea-sure that can alter the course of our lives. Adam and Eve, our roots sold out because they were deceived into wanting something that Satan made them believe that God could not or would not provide. They had that sudden urge to join the ranks of deity, not be like God, but to be as God. Satan moves in slowly, but effectively and causes Adam and Eve to turn their backs on God, thereby loosing the innocence from which they were born with. First, he moves in with a cure to any objections that we may have. And then he takes the time to create doubt saying, (Gen 3:1) "Did God really mean that or was it a misunderstanding on your part?" Secondly, he shifts our mind away from what is right, and spiritually alters our relationship with God. Then he moves in for the kill, clouding your mind with lies of complete darkness. The Bible contains 1189 chapters, only two chapters speak well of man, all other show the need for salvation. Salvation is the answer to all deception.

Salvation

Since the fall of mankind God has begun a plan of salvation for humans. We need salvation because of the serious trouble or predicament Adam and Eve put us in. Our problems did not start by some earthly means like war, hunger, storms or natural disasters, but from sin, therefore these prime areas of concern can only be answered by the blood of Jesus. It is a spiritual thing and needs to be addressed with this picture in mind that our need for salvation cannot be ignored. God Himself makes salvation a personal aspect and provides the opportunity for each of us to receive it. Isaiah 12:2-4 puts it this way, 2: Behold, God is my salvation; I will trust, and not be afraid: for the LORD JEHOVAH is my strength and my song; He also is become my salvation. 3: Therefore, with joy shall ye draw water out of the wells of salvation? 4: And in that day shall ye say, Praise the LORD. Anyone that love or care for you will want you to come into the salvation of the Lord Jesus, because there is none other name whereby to be saved.

CHAPTER 3

Unity

—⧘—

When we glance at the book of Ephesians and take into account the passion that Paul had for the body of Christ and how much he desires unification among the saints, it is not hard to believe that unanimity as signifying in the terms of his letter to the Ephesians was of specificity. In chapters 1-3 He paints the picture of how we can and must become unified with Christ. In chapters 4-6 in that same vivid canvas works to show how the body of Christ should be as one in the church. Here, we have two concerns, the unification of the people with Christ, and the union of the church.

We as Christians must dwell together as a single body of believers in Christ. Psalms 133:1(KJV) says that "It is good and pleasant when brothers live together in unity." So what is Unity, and how can we achieve it? Unity starts in the mind; it is a state of oneness, that quality of togetherness that gives the body of believers a single purpose. And that single purpose causes us to stay focused on Jesus as our Lord and savior, in addition to keeping the church on one accord. All of the parts must function as one. The perfect model of the Church that depicts the sum total of all the parts working as one unit is the Trinity, (Father, Son, and Holy Spirit.)

The gospel of John in chapter 1 shows the God head or trinity as one perfect unit. John 1 puts it this way. In the beginning was the Word, and the Word was with God, and the

Word was God). The three are one. Therefore, in Ephesians Paul is showing us a true picture of what it means to be on one accord, and how important it is to submit to the spiritual authority of the men and women that God has ordained and placed over us. Further, oneness or unity is a spirit of togetherness where we all work for the common good to accomplish the will of God. Jesus made it clear on more than one occasion that He did only the will of the Father. When we are truly unified as one, our relationship change, and become unconditional love for one another.

Relationships bond people closer together or push them further apart. The stronger the relationship, the greater the bond, sometimes the bond is strong enough to cause individuals to overlook the bad in a person and focus only on the divine love that brought them together. This kind of relationship is full of adoration and forgiveness. It is the model setting that God has planned for His people. We must have that special spiritual connection that binds us with each other, and with God. This coming together has benefits; it keeps us from experiencing the feeling of being alone and lost without love. God is always there, all we need to do is call on His name, and he will heal the wounds in our lives. God's expression of love is like a chain that links us together as the core focus for divine unity in the church. Without spiritual blessing and divine love for one another there is no unity.

Spiritual Blessing is one of the initial ways the Lord have chosen to unify human form with Himself, this blessing can only come from above. They are a free gift to mankind that provides all of whatever we need to receive and keep salvation. He has chosen to send us Jesus Christ that we may be adopted as His children. The adoption gives us the right to these blessings. Here, you may ask, what are the blessings? There are two categories of blessings; the blessing that we need and want to maintain life on earth, and the higher blessing that is given to us for the purpose of obtaining eternal life with Christ.

Ephesians 1: 3-7

"3 Praise be to the God and Father of our Lord Jesus Christ, who has blessed us in the heavenly realms with every spiritual blessing in Christ. 4 For he chose us in him before the creation of the world to be holy and blameless in his sight. In love 5 he predestined us to be adopted as his sons through Jesus Christ, in accordance with his pleasure and will— 6 to the praise of his glorious grace, which he has freely given us in the one he loves. 7 In him we have redemption through his blood, the forgiveness of sins, in accordance with the riches of God's grace."

Oneness in Christ is important because it is God that provides every spiritual blessing necessary for forgiveness of sin and foster salvation for eternal life with Him in heaven. "Blessed be the God and Father of our Lord Jesus Christ, who has blessed us with every spiritual blessing."(Eph 1:3)

Understanding Our Relationship to Christ

Relationship defined:

The way we view and interact with each other is constantly being redefined. The inevitability of mutual understanding, communication, and our modern life style offers an adequate explanation of just what we mean by relationship. Since this book is about the occasion of man, it is fitting to develop a picture of relationships as they were from the very beginning of the world. In the beginning God saw that Adam did not have anyone and was lonely, therefore, He created Adam a companion. (Genesis 2:18 (KJV) 18) And the LORD God said, It is not good that the man should be alone; I will make him a help mate for him.) With his companion (woman) Adam began to experience strange, but good and wonderful feelings, he wanted closeness, he wanted sexual pleasure, he wanted a relationship. As a result of his relationship with Eve, the first family emerges.

The emergence of families created new attachment of closeness and loyalty in relationships toward one another. The parents and children formed a special bond of inter-woven feelings strong enough to cause a family member to jeopardize his/her safety to ensure the security and well-being of their loved one's. This is the way God feels about his family on earth, He loves us so much (John 3:16) that he gave his only begotten Son that we may not perish.

Although we look at the initial family relationships as being a fabric strongly knitted together, there are factors that could influence the outcome of relationships. Those factors are skewed in accordance to our value system (Randolph A. Pohlman, Ph.D. Value Driven Management). The things we value most tend to shape our decision making process. For example, we are made by God (Genesis 1:26, John 1:3) and adopted into his family, but the value we placed on wanting to become like God, knowing good and evil (Genesis 3:5) caused us to lose that relationship with God and come under a powerful curse (Genesis 3:14-24). The curse placed upon man caused his entire nature to change, from the innocent peaceful pleasure seeking garden keeper, to the sinful, back-biting, unsatisfied factory worker living by the sweat of his face (Genesis 3:19). So now we ask the question, what is a relationship?

Relationship is (Ephesians cp. 1-3) that indispensable bonds of unity, and the configuration of our interaction with God, government, and the family. All relationships need something to bond them closer together, and with man in connection to God, that one thing is our communication. When we communicate with God in total praise and adorations, we are able to make our request known and ask for guidance. It is these times of which the great hymns like (Faith Review and Expectations) Amazing Grace speaks, to lift our utterances to God Almighty (Robert J. Morgan, Hymn Stories, p78, 2003). Jesus words to His disciples are to be instant in season and out of season, always praying. Pray in the morning, at mealtime giving thanks for your food, or any reason you choose. Prayer is another way we seal our belief, it is a private message between only you and God. God knows if your communication is actually sincere, and the extent of your interest for praying. Since the time of Seth when men began to call upon the Lord, we have made our petition either indirectly, or directly. We made our prayers known in-directly to God during Old Testament times via the priest, however, now because of what Jesus has done, we can relate directly to God. Some of the ways we relate to Christ are via covenant, rituals, and our deliverance.

The Covenant Relationship

It would be nice to be able to be in charge of everything that occurs in and around your person; however we must give considerations to the right and needs of those in proximity to us. If we could set the rules and everyone would just follow what we say, things would be so good. Now we know that this is just a dream because in reality everyone deserves some degree of equality. Equality and fairness is the reason that people with common interest come into covenant agreement with each other. So what is a covenant?

Basically a covenant is a contract or agreement that spells out the terms and conditions to do something, discontinue doing something, or not start an activity or project in exchange for something that has value. If one side of the contract is not performed or breached, then the solutions defined in the agreement for making one whole is executed.

What is valuable to humans or to God? To humans, if you are thinking our eternal salvation, then you are on the right track. This is what we have to gain from a relationship with Jesus. On the other side of the contract is God, and what does He see as value. God see our obedience and praise as valuable, and for that He is offering eternal salvation to all who will properly align themselves in covenant agreement with Him.

In light of this book, our discussion about covenant shall begin at the beginning with the first covenant. The first covenant **(Genesis 6:18 (KJV)** [18] **But with thee will I establish my covenant; and thou shalt come into the ark, thou, and thy sons, and thy wife, and thy sons' wives with thee.)** was God's promise to Noah to save his family during the flood. Noah in turn did his part in warning the people about the flood and building the Ark. However, people do not like bad news; therefore, they did not listen or believe anything would happen, until it was excessively late. God continues to make covenants with his people, take for example Abram. After the death of Terah, his father, God told him to move into his blessing. Abram blessing was not in Haran, but in the promises of God. God made that covenant with Abram to provide blessing and protection for mankind.

Genesis 12:1-3 (KJV) [1] Now the LORD had said unto Abram, Get thee out of thy country, and from thy kindred, and from thy father's house, unto a land that I will shew thee: [2] And I will make of thee a great nation, and I will bless thee, and make thy name great; and thou shalt be a blessing: [3] And I will bless them that bless thee, and curse him that curseth thee: and in thee shall all families of the earth be blessed.

Already we can see that the covenants in both cases are initiated by God. These relations are conditional and eternal. Just because God wants to bless us, don't think that there is a free ride. There is no free ride because in every case God initiates the terms of the relationship, and the terms are "His Terms." In response to God's covenant to Noah; Noah builds the Ark. In response to God's covenant with Abraham; Abraham believed God and it was counted to him as righteousness. Although these covenants were made with and individual, they were for the benefit of all mankind.

In the Bible we can readily see that most covenant are made on behalf of a group, however, God does make personal covenant with his peoples and for the benefit of that person only.

"Isaiah 38:1-5 (KJV) – In those days was Hezekiah sick unto death. And Isaiah the prophet the son of Amoz came unto him, and said unto him, Thus saith the LORD, Set thine house in order: for thou shalt die, and not live. 2 Then Hezekiah turned his face toward the wall, and prayed unto the LORD, 3 And said, Remember now, O LORD, I beseech thee, how I have walked before thee in truth and with a perfect heart, and have done that which is good in thy sight. And Hezekiah wept sore. 4 Then came the word of the LORD to Isaiah, saying, 5 Go, and say to Hezekiah, Thus saith the LORD, the God of David thy father, I have heard thy prayer, I have seen thy tears: behold, I will add unto thy days fifteen years."

As previously stated, if one side of the contact fails to honor the covenant, then remedies are due to the injured party. We as humans have failed, and God loves us so much that He allowed Jesus to cure our note. In His plan of salvation, God sends a savior. Jesus is a savior that will renew and forgive us of our sins as often as we come to Him and substitute his righteousness for our sin.

Rituals

What is the first thought that come to your mind when you hear the word scapegoat. We use this word in many ways and qualify it in as many ways as we use it. However, most people think of it as being a substitute that takes the place of our inadequacies; our fall guy, something or someone able withstand the rage of life and act as our kinsmen redeemer. "Isaiah 53:6 (KJV) [6]All we like sheep have gone astray; we have turned everyone to his own way; and the LORD hath laid on him the iniquity of us all. "God has said that we are not walking in accordance to His will or to His ways and are not able to go on bond for ourselves. We need a savior, someone to be that bearer of sin on our behalf, and we have, in Jesus our justification for eternal life. "Isaiah 53:4 (KJV) [4]Surely he hath borne our griefs, and carried our sorrows: yet we did esteem him stricken, smitten of God, and afflicted."

During our men's Sunday School discussion, we talked about Atonement on both sides of the cross and showed the contrast and correlation. For the purpose of discussion our scripture references was based on Old Testament History Lev. 16. During Old Testament times, God knew that mankind needed saving as much as today. Therefore, He provided Aaron, the high priest a way to atone for the sins of himself first, his family, and Israel. "Leviticus 16:3 (KJV) [3]Thus shall Aaron come into the Holy place: with a young bullock for a sin offering, and a ram for a burnt offering." After the sacrifice is done, then Aaron uses a live goat to take the sins out of the camp.

Old Testament Times	After Christ
"Leviticus 16:21-23 (KJV) 21 And Aaron shall lay both his hands upon the head of the live goat, and confess over him all the iniquities of the children of Israel, and all their transgressions in all their sins, putting them upon the head of the goat, and shall send him away by the hand of a fit man into the wilderness: 22 And the goat shall bear upon him all their iniquities unto a land not inhabited: and he shall let go the goat in the wilderness. 23 And Aaron shall come into the tabernacle of the congregation, and shall put off the linen garments, which he put on when he went into the Holy place, and shall leave them there: "	Romans 10:10 (KJV) [10] For with the heart man believeth unto righteousness; and with the mouth confession is made unto salvation. Romans 10:9 (KJV) [9]That if thou shalt confess with thy mouth the Lord Jesus, and shalt believe in thine heart that God hath raised him from the dead, thou shalt be saved. Romans 6:9 (KJV) [9] Knowing that Christ being raised from the dead dieth no more; death hath no more dominion over him.

This illustration prophesies the coming of Christ and depicts how He would bear our sins. The death of the bull and goat give a picture of what Jesus must suffer for us and the scapegoat signifies the resurrection of Jesus bearing all of our iniquities and shortcomings. Once Jesus freed us of our sins, we are no longer under bondage. Our sins are both forgiven and forgotten. Hebrews 8:12 (KJV) [12] For I will be merciful to their unrighteousness, and their sins and their iniquities will I remember no more.

The Ascension

On the other side of the cross the high priest and only the high priest, would enter into the most Holy place, taking the blood that he offered for himself and for the sins that the people committed in ignorance (Hebrews 9:7). Once the ceremony was finished; the scapegoat took their sins away into the land of forgetfulness, to be remembered no more. However, on this side of the cross, things are different. Jesus is raised for our justification to finalize our salvation and open the doors of heaven to us forever. Christ said over and over "My body is the temple." Christ, as Aaron went in the presence of God through the veil, to make atonement for our sins. For Aaron's veil was made of fabric, and for Jesus' veil was His flesh. His dying on the cross removes the veil and His Ascension opened the heavens once and for all John 2:18-21 (KJV), and redeemed us with His own blood (Hebrews 9:12).

John 2:18-21 (KJV) [18]Then answered the Jews and said unto him, What sign shewest thou unto us, seeing that thou doest these things? [19]Jesus answered and said unto them, Destroy this temple, and in three days I will raise it up. [20]Then said the Jews, Forty and six years was this temple in building, and wilt thou rear it up in three days? [21]But he spake of the temple of his body.

People on both sides of the cross need Atonement, however on this side Jesus being the perfect sacrifice has paid it all and there is no need for the yearly sacrament. Jesus was our supreme substitute. What is a substitute? A substitute is a replacement or stand-in. Consider this, the museums have replica of expensive art displayed when it is not safe to exhibit that one of a kind painting. In the movies we have substitutes called doubles, which stand in for the real star when the scenes become too dangerous. From these basic examples, we can safely conclude that the world see a substitute as being a substandard or expendable replacement for the genuine article. However in reality, we as Christians know that Jesus is our substitute. He is the one who took our place on the cross and died for the sins of the world.

And because Jesus has paid the ultimate price, we are now free from the sting of sin and death, Satan is defeated. But Satan has not given up on his mission to confuse you about where you stand in Christ. We were saved then, now and on into eternity. God's plan of salvation is for anyone willing to accept Him as their Lord and Savior; to have eternal life. Jesus is our substitute, because He is the good Shepherd.

The Good Shepherd

In the Christian community, followers are labeled as sheep. The master of the sheep is the one who is charged with the health and well being of the flock. This Shepherd must process all of the traits lacking in the sheep fold. Sheep by nature are not the sharpest animals on the farm. The nature and attributes of a sheep are (not inclusive) as follows: Sheep are social animals, timid, docile, usually experience degrees of anxiety when left alone, need constant protection from everything including themselves, love to over eat sometimes to the point of death. Therefore, sheep have limited intelligence and sense of direction which is the cause of many problems for them, and because they are the way they are; they need constant guidance. Jesus is the good Shepherd that provides guidance for all who will receive Him. So what makes Jesus the good Shepherd?

Jesus has said, I will never leave you nor forsake you. He says this because He has a stake in us. We are His inheritance as indicated in (Ephesians 1:18 (KJV) [18] The eyes of your understanding being enlightened; that ye may know what is the hope of his calling, and what the riches of the glory of his inheritance in the saints). And because we are his inheritance He will go that extra mile to ensure our safety and well being as opposed to a hired hand. The owner (Jesus) will fight off the predators (Satan and his camp), while the hired hand is more interest in his or her own safety. This is the primary reason that Jesus can boldly own the statement "I am the good Shepherd." John 10:14 (KJV) [14] I am the good shepherd, and know my sheep, and am known of mine.

We know by both our faith and works of Jesus that He is indeed the good Shepherd.

CHAPTER 4

Deliverance

—⁓—

The Law and Grace

The Bible is composed of two interdependent sets of guidance for His people, the Old Testament which was based on the law, and the New Testament that is based on grace. John 1:17 (KJV) [17] For the law was given by Moses, but grace and truth came by Jesus Christ. At this point is helpful to define our position on these topics; the Law, and Grace. First we shall discuss the Law.

The Law

What is law and how does it function? For the purpose of this book, we are concerned with the Law as it applies to the Bible. So, then what is the Law? The Law is a set of guidelines or rules that are used to measure acceptable conduct. These statutes are designed to set the minimum satisfactory standards for behavior, and prescribe remedies for person or persons that do not meet the standards. For example, In Old Testament times, God tells us in the Leviticus Law that you are not to have sexual relationship with mankind, as with womankind: it is abomination. And the remedy for disobeying that Law is death. Leviticus 20:13 (KJV) [13] If a man also lie with mankind, as he lieth with a woman, both of them have committed an abomination: they shall surely be put to death; their blood shall be upon them. On the other hand, let's consider a more current example; you are in your vehicle driving down the freeway, and notice that the speed limit is posted at 50 miles per hour. However, you are late for work and need to drive faster than the posted limits to punch the clock on time; the instant your vehicle travels faster than 50 miles you are not incompliance with the rules of the road. If you are caught by the police, remedies in the form of a ticket are assessed.

Now that we have briefly described a basic function of the law, it is time to make a clear picture of its doctrine, what the law could and could not do, why we fail the law, and what God did to remedy our failure. The basic functions of the law as denoted in Old Testament doctrine sets the rules for all of the social and spiritual activity of the Jews until it fulfillment by Jesus. Until the revelation or manifestation of Jesus, the Law was it. It was first given to Moses in the book of Exodus on Mount Sinai, beginning with the Ten Commandments. The Ten Commandments lay out the rules of how we should reverence and have respect for God, and how we should treat one another.

"Exodus 20:1-21 (KJV) **(Rules to have a relationship with God)**[4] Thou shalt not make unto thee any graven image, or any likeness of anything that is in Heaven above, or that is in the earth beneath, or that is in the water under the earth: [5] Thou shalt not bow down thyself to them, nor serve them: for I the LORD thy God am a jealous God, visiting the iniquity of the fathers upon the children unto the third and fourth generation of them that hate me; [6] And shewing mercy unto thousands of them that love me, and keep my commandments. [7] Thou shalt not take the name of the LORD thy God in vain; for the LORD will not hold him guiltless that taketh his name in vain. [8] Remember the sabbath day, to keep it holy. [9] Six days shalt thou labour, and do all thy work: [10] But the seventh day is the sabbath of the LORD thy God: in it thou shalt not do any work, thou, nor thy son, nor thy daughter, thy manservant, nor thy maidservant, nor thy cattle, nor thy stranger that is within thy gates: [11] For in six days the LORD made heaven and earth, the sea, and all that in them is, and rested the seventh day: wherefore the LORD blessed the sabbath day, and hallowed it. [12] **(The way we should relate each other)** Honour thy father and thy mother: that thy days may be long upon the land which the LORD thy God giveth thee. [13] Thou shalt not kill. [14] Thou shalt not commit adultery. [15] Thou shalt not steal. [16] Thou shalt not bear false witness against thy neighbour. [17] Thou shalt not covet thy neighbour's house, thou shalt not covet thy neighbour's wife, nor his manservant, nor his maidservant, nor his ox, nor his ass, nor any thing that is thy neighbour's.

Following the Ten Commands we have the Law of Moses (Exodus 20-24), the Prophets (major and minor), and the Law of David (Psalm) "Luke 24:44 (KJV) [44] And he said unto them, These are the words which I spake unto you, while I was yet with you, that all things must be fulfilled, which were written in the law of Moses, and in the prophets, and in the psalms, concerning me." Jesus said it all; the law was not designed, or intended for the salvation of man. It was given to us to show us how much we needed and depended on Jesus. However, there are things that the law could do for us like set moral standards, establish a code of conduct for morality and immorality, and protect the sanctity of the family. Whereas there is one thing that it could not do, and that one thing is; to save man from his sin. Romans 8:3-4 (KJV) [3] For what the law could not do, in that it was weak through the flesh, God sending his own Son in the likeness of sinful flesh, and for sin, condemned sin in the flesh: [4] That the righteousness of the law might be fulfilled in us, who walk not after the flesh, but after the Spirit. This is the reason that we failed under the law, however God had a remedy. The remedy is His Son Jesus. And Jesus tells us that we still have rules, and on His rules hang both the Law and the Prophets. That rule or law is to love our neighbor as ourselves, and to love God with all our heart, soul, mind, and strength. No matter how hard we try, we can never live up to the law, but it did give us promise until the coming of Jesus to make the rules just right. Jesus rewrites the rules, because often we fall short and need grace.

Grace

Even though the word grace is broad brushed across the pages of both the Old and New Testaments, we seem to make the disassociation between grace and the law. When the spin doctor speaks of under grace, somehow they end up describing them as being mutually exclusive. They say it's the scripture, well if it is, we will soon find out. We know that God does bestow his grace upon the lives of each and every one of us daily. It is given without cost or obligation (**KJV** Matt 5:45) God sends his rain on the just as well as the unjust. Everyone gets to benefit from the grace of God.

What is Grace
In my investigation of both the Old Testament and New Testament, grace is treated in the same fashion; it is described as favor. In more specific terms, it is favor unmerited. Unmerited favor is a free gift; our salvation fits into the category of unmerited favor. We as humans did nothing and cannot do anything that would make us worthy of salvation. God has given it to us because (**KJV** John 3:16) He so loved the world that He has extended the greatest form of grace anyone can receive. He gave the life of His only begotten son that we may have a right to the tree of life. Our salvation is purchased by the grace of God through Jesus

Christ. We can literally see the hands of God as they provide grace to us. We are undeserving but, starting with Adam and following throughout the history of man, grace as Paul puts it does abound.

In the Old Testament God's grace is first shown to Adam. The first need for grace is because of his disobedience. After Adam fell to sin God showed him grace by covering his shame with clothing and provided a way out of his sin through the sacrifice of Jesus. Another example not so far away is illustrated in the life of Noah. In **KJV** Genesis 6:8 Noah and his family was saved because Noah found favor in the eyes of the Lord. So thus far, the color of grace seem to sparkle with those gleaming effects of unmerited favor, which encompass thankfulness; forgiveness, and justification, to round out its meaning. Is there more, of course in some cases when we receive grace as did Noah, we need the strength and understanding to endure until grace has run its full course. I am certain that Noah required vast amounts of enduring strength in order to manage the Ark during the storm. Likewise we need additional support in receiving some measures of grace that God provides for us today. For example; if God has given you the grace to become a Medical Doctor, then you would need additional help in reaching that goal. God would also need to grant you the patience to study for long periods, and the strength to perform surgery on and individual. In this light, grace takes on a new meaning altogether. Grace is the unmerited favor given to us by God along with the strength and support necessary for us to receive it. Because we receive grace from God, and our sins are forever covered by the blood of Jesus, we are justified. Our justification makes us once again in the image of God through the blood of His Son Jesus Christ, and because we are Christ like we must extend grace to those around us.

Showing Grace

The old adage "The hardest job that you have ever done is the one that you do not know to do" applies here as well. In order to show grace, you must have it, you would be seriously challenged to give something that you do not have. By the gift of God we have or walk in grace, and because we have grace we must share with others the good news of our salvation. **(KJV)** Ephesians 2:5 [5] Even when we were dead in sins, hath quickened us together with Christ, (by grace ye are saved;) We are saved through grace **(KJV)** Ephesians 2:8-10 [8] For by grace are ye saved through faith; and that not of yourselves: it is the gift of God: [9] Not of works, lest any man should boast. [10] For we are his workmanship, created in Christ Jesus unto good works, which God hath before ordained that we should walk in them. In the scripture above God is telling us that grace comes only form Him, it does not come by your ability to purchase it, repent for it, studied for it or earned it. To receive salvation or to be saved you must accept Jesus as Lord and Savior. As Christians, we are compelled to bring the good news about how people can be saved. Some churches do it within the boundaries of the sanctuary, others expand to include outreach teams, and mission field representatives.

As a Christian whether acting as an outreach person on a mission team, or on your Job from time to time someone in your path will infringe upon your right or come against you wrongly. When this happens you must have enough grace to forgive that person. Consider this, at my place of business; the time comes when we must sign up to be placed on the overtime list, if and only if we want to work overtime during the next quarter. I placed my name on the list close to what I thought was the end of the tolerance period. A few days later, some of my co-workers ask if I had placed my name on the list timely. A grievance was filed against me through the union. I was called in and asked by management if my name was post timely also. I said yes, but my investigation reveals that I did sign the list late, and that everyone whose name appeared on the overtime list was also posted late. The list was supposed to be posted on 1 September and removed on 17 September, but management did not put the list until 20 September therefore, the union ruled that all name on the list would stay. Some of the people who grieved my signing do not speak or talk to me, but I must forgive them. Paul says that if no law is broken then there is no need for grace, but when the infraction does occur, we must stand ready and willing to forgive. God is just to forgive me; I therefore must do the same, because my forgiveness does not depend on what others may or may not do. Forgiveness is one of the detours that keep us from traveling down the road of sin.

Grace and Sin

If you have ever played the game of monopoly there comes a time when you may roll the dice to just the right number or pull the correct card needed to land in jail. However, some immediately move to "just visiting" because they have a "get out of jail free card." Grace is not that get out of jail card free for sin card. Just because we are under grace does not give us the right to do anything we want, and then expect to play the grace card as a way out. Professor Johnson, my ethic instructor said during one of his lectures, that standards never change. We may change the way we look at the laws, and stop using it, but it's still there. For example, we know that it is wrong to kill, destroy others property, rape someone, or drive without a driver's license; just because we come up with a new law saying that we can now do these things, does not make it right. If it was wrong then, it is still wrong. Jesus says that He is the only way to the Father, and that there is no other way. We cannot change that standard Jesus has set forth because it is now fashionable or politically correct to show tolerance to other religions. When Jesus made this statement it was true, guess what; it still is. Jesus yet the only way and that will not change.

Is grace and the law mutually exclusive

To answer the question of whether or not grace and the law have nothing in common we only need to go to Galatians chapter 5. **(KJV)** Galatians 5:4-6 [4] Christ is become of no effect unto you, whosoever of you are justified by the law; ye are fallen from grace. [5] For we through the Spirit wait for the hope of righteousness by faith. [6] For in Jesus Christ neither circumcision availeth anything, nor uncircumcision, but faith which worketh by love. What is Paul saying here? Is he telling us that grace does away with the law? Of course not, he is talking about our justification. Our justification through Jesus is what makes us free from sin and reconciled to God. Therefore, he is saying that if you think that the good deeds you perform are your ticket to heaven, then your justi-fication is subject to the penalty of the law. The law is holy and written equally to our justification, but we as humans are unable to live up to the Holy Scriptures and if the law is what we are depending on, we are lost because the Law has no room for error. Therefore, the law and grace is not in opposition, but if you use the law as justification, then your judgment shall be measured via the Law.

Unity in the Church

Relationship of Christians with the unbeliever

When we think of unity between Christian and the nonbeliever, we must consider how the Bible says that it should exist between us. Jesus said that unity is only found through him, he is the bread of life and that we must accept him into our lives. We must believe in his death and resur-rection for our salvation. "John 6:48-51 (NASB95) [48] "I am the bread of life. [49] "Your fathers ate the manna in the wilderness, and they died. [50] "This is the bread which comes down out of heaven, so that one may eat of it and not die. [51] "I am the living bread that came down out of heaven; if anyone eats of this bread, he will live forever; and the bread also which I will give for the life of the world is My flesh." As Christian, (John 17:11) we are to take care of God's people just as he takes care of us. Jesus often discussed with his disciples the value of love and illustrated to them how it was the source of nourishment for both the soul and physical being of an individual. When we feed our unsaved brother with love, it serves to bring them closer to us that we may introduce them to Christ. Salvation is for everyone. "Isaiah 55:1 (KJV) [1] Ho, every one that thirtieth, come ye to the waters, and he that hath no money; come ye, buy, and eat; yea, come, buy wine and milk without money and without price." God extends salvation to everyone as a free gift and we must do the same. Non-believers are depicted as people feeding off of food that has no nutritional value, and they continue to spend their resources on thing that will not satisfy them. The world cannot satisfy the void in a person life, only God can fulfill that need. God offers a free gift without cost (Milk and Wine a symbol of blessing), but it does come with obligations. We are obligated to love everyone, to pray and intercede on their behalf.

CHAPTER 5

—ɯ—

Prayer

—∿—

What is Prayer?

If you have ever had the need to talk with God, your direct line to Him was through prayer. Then prayer is the name that we give to communicating one on one, or talking with God. Just think about the way we communicate with one another. We have basically three mode or methods by which we deliver messages. They are verbal, non verbal, and written. Verbal communication is delivered via speech or audio means, non-verbal communication is conveyed via our body language, and written communication is via letters and symbols that make up intelligence such as words and pictures. When we are talking to each other, our body language must also match what we are saying in order for the communication to be congruent. If we are on the phone, and the person to whom we are speaking cannot see us, have no way of knowing what our body language is like. Therefore the communication is incongruent.

However, this is not the case with God; He is always with you and knows the very intent of your heart. When you ask for forgiveness of your sin, and to be cleanse from them He is right there to answer Acts 3:19 (GW) [19] So change the way you think and act, and turn {to God} to have your sins removed. When you go to Him with the burdens and cares of

Love Lifted me 9/18/09 Cracker Barrell
Jeff

the world prayer is the answer. 1 Peter 5:7 (KJV) Casting all
your care upon him; for he careth for you. Prayer then is our
protection; that's the reason it is so important. In Ephesians
6:18 (KJV) [18] Praying always with all prayer and supplication
in the Spirit, and watching thereunto with all perseverance
and supplication for all saints; Paul point out the importance of prayer and tell us that we cannot be lazy. Prayer is
a continuous spiritual interaction with our Heavenly Father
that sometimes requires more than just the five minutes per
day you are willing to spend during your spare time. Prayer
in some cases requires you to wait for your break through.
Why should we be so patience in waiting for our answer;
because we have an assiduous hard working enemy in the
devil? The devil is shrewd and always plotting your downfall, this is the reason v 12 tell us to be mindful of the Devil's
tricks. Jesus has already done the hard part, but could you
continue your communication with Him for one hour, one
day, one week, or however long it takes, to get your answer.

Answered prayer is our spiritual capital, and the resources
for our physical satisfaction. Everything we need both spiritual and physical can be obtained through prayer. In the book
of James, we find that all we have to do is ask God for what
we need and He is willing and able to supply all of them.
However, we go lacking for many things simply because we
will not ask James 4:2-3 (KJV) [2] Ye lust, and have not: ye
kill, and desire to have, and cannot obtain: ye fight and war,
yet ye have not, because ye ask not. [3] Ye ask, and receive
not, because ye ask amiss, that ye may consume it upon your
lusts. There are many times, that I will start a project that I
have to pray for the wisdom and knowledge to complete the
activity. And ever further, I go in prayer asking God to tell
help me with such things as: where my keys are, give me
the message I need to convey to my Sunday School Class,
give me the wisdom to solve small conflicts on the job, and
for God to increase my spiritual understanding. All of this

is well and good, and God will answer. However, if I ask with the wrong motives to benefit the lust of my flesh only; those prayers will go unanswered. Jesus spent much time in prayer; in fact the majority of His time was spent in prayer. The Father answered, because He was praying the will of the Father. The will of the Father defines the criterions whereby we may obtain the assets we need from God. And the time we spend praying is our kingdom investment for these gifts. Our investment spends on both sides of the coin. On one side is faith the other doubt. James 1:6-7 (KJV) [6] But let him ask in faith, nothing wavering. For he that wavereth is like a wave of the sea driven with the wind and tossed. [7] For let not that man think that he shall receive any thing of the Lord. If we ask in faith we shall receive, whereas praying in doubt and uncertainty cause our prayer to go unanswered.

What is it that we need from God? To be short and to the point, we need mercy and grace. But in order to get mercy and grace, we must come into the presence of God. Jesus said, Matthew 11:28 (KJV) [28] Come unto me, all ye that labour and are heavy laden, and I will give you rest. That is a prescription for prayer, and in order to receive the full benefits of prayer we must know how to pray.

How to Pray?

How to, is one of the most important aspects of any activity in your life? Consider this, one of the presents I got for Christmas was a portable lab top computer desk (from my daughter Kesha) with printer stand. The picture of it on the box was so beautiful. But when I opened that box, it was in what seemed to be a million pieces. It had screws of different sizes and shapes, little flat things that did something, and round knobs that just did not seem to go anywhere. But with all of those pieces was a set of instruction. Instruction that told you what all came in the box, and the type of tools needed to assemble it. Without those instruction that beautiful

Have faith in God! This is the will of God.

table would still be unassembled parts. Just as I was in need of guidance to fit all of the parts together for my portable computer table, we also need guidance in our prayer life.

The Bible is our primary source of information or our instruction manual on the things of God. In today's information age we have vast interactive source to help us understand the instructions given in the Bible. Some of the most common sources are electronic Bibles, the internet, our pastor, and other Christian mentors and most importantly The Holy Spirit. The Bible is not an easy book to read or understand, just as some manuals are not. In some manuals the instructions are so complicated that the manufacture put in graphically illustrations and pictures to get us through the project. And as a last resort, if we still do not understand how all those things fit together, they provide you with an 800 phone number or website knowledge portal.

God treats you the same way in the Bible. He gives us step by step instruction as to how to pray Matthew 6:5 (KJV) (5 And when thou prayest, thou shalt not be as the hypocrites are: For they love to pray standing in the synagogues and in the corners of the streets, that they may be seen of men. Verily I say unto you, They have their reward). And then paints a picture of each step necessary to gain His presence Matthew 6:6 (KJV) 6 But thou, when thou prayest, enter into thy closet, and when thou hast shut thy door, pray to thy Father which is in secret; and thy Father which seeth in secret shall reward thee openly. If the instructions are too hard in the Bible, He gives us officers that we can go to for help, but it is The Holy Spirit that teaches us the deeper meaning. The Holy Spirit lets us know how to talk to God. When we talk to God our conversation must be from the very depth of our heart. Jesus gave us a model of how we should pray. Matthew 6:9-13 (KJV) 9 After this manner therefore pray ye: Our Father which art in heaven, Hallowed be thy name. 10 Thy kingdom come. Thy will be done in earth, as it is in heaven. 11 Give us

STePS iN praying to the Father

① Reverance God
② Worship God
③ PRAISE God

this day our daily bread. [12] And forgive us our debts, as we forgive our debtors. [13] And lead us not into temptation, but deliver us from evil: In this model He taught his disciples how they should communicate with and come into the presence of God. He starts out telling that they should reverence God by coming into His presence with praise and worship. Praise is what we do to get into the presence of God, and worship is what we do when we get there, (Dr. Randolph Bracy, Jr., Pastor (New Covenant Baptist Church of Orlando). Jesus was not trying to give them a cookie cut prayer to say over and over every time they prayed, but rather an understanding of all the essential elements of prayer. Equipped with this information or model of prayer, we are able to be more effective in both our private and public prayer life.

When we pray our prayers must be directed to God and not to be seen of men, but in supplication and the giving of thanks. The prayer model starts off in supplication; which means to worship in the present of power and bend our knees before the almighty God and thanking God for all of the blessing that He is bestowing upon us. There are times when we are not able to pray for ourselves and need someone to go to God on our behalf. When someone else or you pray for another person needs, this is called prayer of intercession. Jesus fulltime job is to make intercession for us daily. He has taken our sin upon Himself and cleaned us from all unrighteousness and presents us as holy before God our Father. Jesus is our intercessor, the one Who entreat God to save us from the ultimate punishment, and because this is His role, we must pray in the name of Jesus.

In the name of Jesus

If you have had the opportunity to visit any churches, and hear the person that is delivering the prayer; usually they begin and end the prayer by saying "In the name of Jesus." Jesus said that we are to pray in His name. John

14:13-14 (KJV) [13] And whatsoever ye shall ask in my name, that will I do, that the Father may be glorified in the Son. [14] If ye shall ask any thing in my name, I will do it. And as a result our request will be answered. However, just by adding Jesus name to your prayer does not mean praying in the name of Jesus. Praying in the name of Jesus means to pray the will of God; therefore it is not so much the words we use, but that the purpose in our heart is in agreement with God. It is the will of God that we recognize the authority of Jesus as being His Son, with all power. Jesus has the power over death as our resurrected savior. Romans 1:4-5 (KJV) [4] And declared to be the Son of God with power, according to the spirit of holiness, by the resurrection from the dead: [5] By whom we have received grace and apostleship, for obedience to the faith among all nations, for his name: However, there are times that we need something from God and do not know how to pray for it. These are the times that we need the Holy Spirit.

In the Spirit

Jesus disciples expressed their inability to know how to pray as they should; as a result they went to Jesus and ask for help. Jesus provided help for them, but today we have the Holy Spirit to teach and guide us through effective prayer. Ephesians 6:18 (KJV) [18] Praying always with all prayer and supplication in the Spirit, and watching thereunto with all perseverance and supplication for all saints; Like soldiers, Christians are to be continually alert, praying in the spirit (Minister Barbara Woods, The Life Center Church, Bible study). Praying in the spirit is the operative words, because the Holy Spirit knows the will of God. And to get an answer from God, we must pray his will. However, it is not enough to just pray the will of God; we must also have the faith to believe that we will receive what we ask for. We get and strengthen our faith through studding the Word of God.

Romans 10:17 (KJV) [17] So then faith cometh by hearing, and hearing by the word of God. When we read and study the word, we must also believe it. Our faith comes by believing and believing by the word of God. If you do not believe your prayers will be answered or that God will perform His will in your life, then pray for the wisdom to believe, because prayers unlocks the doors to the mysteries of God (Sophia J. Dawson, my wife)

CHAPTER 6

—◆—

God Reveals His Mysteries

—ɯ—

The Bible begins with the narrative of creation and history of mankind. It unfolds what we think of as hidden knowledge about the world and how we got our start. Genesis 1:1-2 (KJV) [1] In the beginning God created the heaven and the earth. [2] And the earth was without form, and void; and darkness was upon the face of the deep. And the Spirit of God moved upon the face of the waters. Here inward of these verses contains information authorized for disclosure; God wants us to know his great secrets and mysteries. Mysteries as the world would have it, are designed to be held in back or kept unknown and unseen by others until that last and final moment. It is the thing that holds our attention through the full course of a detective story. We can go to the end of the book and find out what the mystery is, but that kind of information lacks detail and juice. Details are what our mind wants. So God give us all of the details of His mysteries right up front. He tells us how the world begins as a mass of confusion, void and without form. There was nothing on earth; God is the creator of everything that is on the earth. Everything we see or do points to our God, Jesus, and the Holy Spirits.

Man is always in search of the answers to the murkiness that looms to evade our intellect, simply because he wants to know the answer to the what(s), and where(s). Jesus facilitates our curiosity about Devine mysteries by teaching in parables. He do this in order to give us a peek at Heavenly meaning via things we already know right here on earth. The deep secrets that would riddle or puzzle our minds are solved for us by Jesus in the teaching of his parables. Matthew 13:17(KJV) [17] For verily I say unto you, That many prophets and righteous men have desired to see those things which ye see, and have not seen them; and to hear those things which ye hear, and have not heard them. Unlike the world, Jesus does not make us wonder or play mind games with us by dropping a clue here and there meant only for the most intelligent peoples to solve. He does not send us down dark alleys or point us in the wrong direction with those red herring clues designed to add difficulty. God does not create problems for us. He gives us the best of the best and grace when we fall short of our best through His son Jesus. We truly have the best of the best; in that does God keep secrets.

God's Secrets

Does God keep secrets, well let's call on some from the not so distant past "Moses" and see what he has to say about the matter. Deuteronomy 29:29 (KJV) [29] The secret things belong unto the LORD our God: but those things which are revealed belong unto us and to our children for ever, that we may do all the words of this law. (Matthew Henry Concise) Realizing how important it is to think that God does not keep secrets from us then find out that He does send shock waves through our natural body. We just do not believe that God would keep something from us. Ok, answer this question, what will happen tomorrow, six hours from now, two minutes from now? If you truly know the answer to these questions, then Play Lotto and come out of the factory. However, on the softer side we are not able to understand why God would keep secrets from us. To keep a secret have the implication of having something to hide. Yes God does have something to hide, but through the Bible He provides private instruction at the personal level to all of His pupils. Therefore, to know the revelation of God's word, you must Read and Pray (Bishop Ronald F. Kimble, Life Center Church, Eatonville FL). When we stay in the Word, and meditate on the Word we learn what the will of God is for our lives.

God will for our lives are two grouping, each being mutually exclusive of the other. God have a perfect will for our lives and a permissive will. The permissive will borderlines His tolerance level for our minimum acceptable behavior, whereas the perfect will of God goes so much further. Consider the Patriarch and fathers of our faith from Noah to Jesus and we can begin to see the unavailing of God's will for His people. With the exception of Jesus, there are times that the seemingly unknowable would be held in secret, and then released via God's prophets at the appointed time (Dr. Kimble). This knowledge was not hidden from the man of God, but guarded carefully from those who were profane in both doctrine and religious teaching. God gives His people revelation knowledge that is incomprehensible for the human intellect via supernatural disclosure (Sophia J. Dawson).

In Old Testament Time during the days of Moses, God unveils or reveals His will on occasions through the use of the Urim and Thummim. . "URIM" is a name that signifies or is derived from: "lights," "fires." **http://define.com/URIM**, and the Thummim is perfection; truth. It was the method that God gave insight to his people **http://define.com/ THUMMIM**. Exodus 28:30 (ASV) [30] And thou shalt put in the breastplate of judgment the Urim and the Thummim; and they shall be upon Aaron's heart, when he goeth in before Jehovah: and Aaron shall bear the judgment of the children of Israel upon his heart before Jehovah continually. By means of the Urim and Thummim God converse with His people and provided solutions to their problems as in the case of King David. David ask God a direct question (1 Samuel 30:8

(ASV) [8] And David inquired of Jehovah, saying, "If I pursue after this troop, shall I overtake them?" and Gods answer was not jaded and permeated with overwhelming details of the battle. It was lucid and simplistic (1 Samuel 30:8 And he answered him, Pursue; for thou shalt surely overtake them, and shalt without fail recover all). However, when we cease to follow the instruction of God and align ourselves with other doctrines our relationship with Him changes (Dr. Kimble). We can no longer here from Him. Consider this, King Saul, King of Israel disobeyed God and was excommunicated. 1 Samuel 28:6 (ASV) [6] When Saul inquired of Jehovah, Jehovah answered him not, neither by dreams, nor by Urim, nor by prophets. King Saul's disobedient was the great downfall that put up a wall of separation shading the real truth and giving way to the mischief prominently of his own strong mind and hard heart. Therefore, he was reduced to seeking answers from others mediums.

Today on this side of the cross we have Jesus as our intercessor and the Holy Spirit to guide us into all truth. And if we should fall, He is right there to comfort us, pick us up, and get us going again. We have all the modern tools necessary to know what God expects from us. In my home we have many Bibles, history and reference books to explain the Bible. Some are the common paper back and others are the electronic media. However, this was not the case for early Christian and other believers predating them. The Bible was an expensive project; it could cost an entire family or household one year's wages to purchase a copy of the ((Old Testament) the Bible Answer Man 1-888-ASK-HANK (275-4265)). However, promises are examples of Gods unveiled mysteries

CHAPTER 7

Forgiveness

The Layout

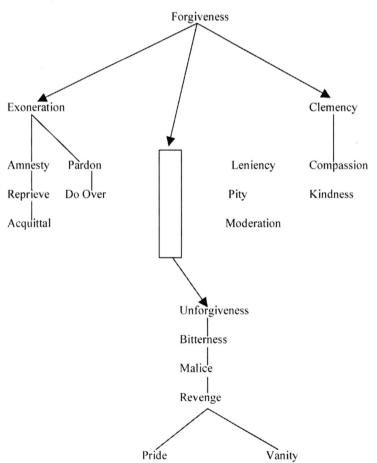

Forgiveness

Exoneration   Clemency

Amnesty   Pardon   Leniency   Compassion

Reprieve   Do Over   Pity   Kindness

Acquittal   Moderation

Unforgiveness

Bitterness

Malice

Revenge

Pride   Vanity

Outline

Forgiveness

Introduction

Define and Purpose of Forgiveness

Categories of Forgiveness

- Exoneration
  o Pardon
  o Acquittal

- Amnesty
  o Do over or second chance
  o Reprieve

- Clemency
  o Leniency
  o Pity
  o Compassion
  o Kindness

Unforgiveness

Bitterness

Malice

Revenge
- Pride
- Vanity

Introduction

God have several tools that he uses to make us more in his image and likeness. And because He made us in His image and put us in charge of everything on earth it is our obligation to love and support all that He tells us to do. Some of the tools are given as special gifts and other are common to all. **1 Corinthians 12:27-30 (KJV)** [27] Now ye are the body of Christ, and members in particular. [28] And God hath set some in the church, first apostles, secondarily prophets, thirdly teachers, after that miracles, then gifts of healings, helps, governments, diversities of tongues. [29] *Are* all apostles? *Are* all prophets? *Are* all teachers? *Are* all workers of miracles? [30] Have all the gifts of healing? Do all speak with tongues? Do all interpret? However this segment of the book will look at the unlisted gift that makes all other's possible. This untitled gift is a crucial for our very salvation. It is the gift of forgiveness.

Forgiveness is a two edge sword that cuts in both directions each edge achieving a vastly different purpose. On one edge is forgiveness, and the other side is Unforgiveness. Forgiveness is of God and Unforgiveness is of Satan camp. Now, because it is our custom to talk about the good first, I will address forgiveness. It is the one gift that can mend the broken hearts and heal the open wounds in our spirit. Therefore it is the nerve center of our being. Jesus taught the disciples how to pray highlighting forgiveness as a must do in order to commune and collaborate with both God and humans. Forgiveness takes into account, grace which means to show unconditional favor to an offender, rather than retaliate with evil. We must forgive our friends, neighbors, and ourselves if we want God to forgive us. God have this forgiveness feature built into us; to release all of those self induced bonds of Satan from our lives. Therefore we can easily conclude that forgiveness is a front runner, on the fore front of spiritual warfare. Just as forgiveness is the front runner for a relationship with Jesus and our salvation, unforgiveness is the front runner for a relationship with Satan and eternal damnation. Consider this short illustration. One of my functions at the Life Center Church is outreach. On occasion I visit with elderly people, in their homes, and at private care facilities. After awhile they will get use to you, they will begin to talk. Some of the stories want a do over. The most common desire for a do over is their stories about unforgiveness. The person that stand out most tell this story (name withheld for privacy), of bitterness in the family. She is a beautifully save individual who loves the Lord with all of her heart. She also loves her family, however somewhere in the not too distant past; problems arose and were not immediately resolved. The major cause of her problem stems from her lifelong desire to become a missionary worker assigned to Africa. This position came available, and she accepted it. However, she would be required to absorb the majority of her expense, with minimum aid from the Church. To make this possible, she sells her home and liquidates the majority of her stock portfolio. Her family was in diametric opposition to her doing this, therefore they discontinue all contact with her. Her husband divorces her; the daughter would not have any contact with her physical or otherwise. She was kept from the grandchildren as well. When she mailed parcels, cards and letters to her grandchildren they were returned with this inscription (Refused, Return to Sender). However over the years, God have brought a healing to that family, and mended the hearts closer together. I could see the power of God working thing out in her life and forgiveness in operation. This week she was so happy (Dec 2008) to tell me that she would for the first time in twelve years see her daughter and grandchildren. As powerful as forgiveness is, unforgiveness has robbed this family of twelve years.

Purpose of Forgiveness

When we are posed with the question about forgiveness, we often think of others in terms of what they must have done to need it. However, there are occasions when we are in direct conflict ourselves and Satan uses those opportunities to put you in bondage. He puts all of those negative thoughts to the front of your mind accusing you to the point that you become bitter with yourself. When this happens we are in trouble and need to forgive ourselves for past events, otherwise we may come to the point that we cause harm to ourselves. So exactly what is forgiveness and the purpose thereof? Before we answer this question it is necessary to recognize the mentality of humans and the way we think. We have the fallacy etched into our minds that forgiveness is something that others need and we are the people that need to forgive them. But in reality, and canned terms it is the grace to resolve that all is well and give others another chance. The person that was wronged is offering a pardon for our trespasses; but the one thing that forgiveness is not is rationalization. Rationalization cause one to fit into the mold of conditional forgiveness. Examples of conditional forgiveness are as follows:

- Well we are Christians therefore we have to forgive them.
- Johnnie is a high strung A+ personality profile so we must forgive him, because that's the way he is.
- Boys and girls are different and boys will be boys.
- Well they are black/white/other and this is what they do, it's their upbringing so they cannot help it.

Forgiveness then is not rationalization, rather it is the ability for one person to realize that the other person who wronged them is not God and is capable of mistakes. We must treat wrongful acts committed against us as just that and as Jesus taught, forgive and get on with life. Getting on with life is the primary purpose for forgiveness.

Categories of Forgiveness

* Exoneration

In the perfect world, the word exoneration need not come up. But because we do not live in that snapped on, plugged in society with all of the reciprocal modifications necessary to keep us from failing; we must learn to let by-gones be by-gones. Constant failure is the one human attribute that you can count on, if there is a way to blow it we will find it, sometime our failure is not entirely all ours. We are blame wrongly for various things, during the course of our growth, development. When this happens and the truth is found out, the wrongly accused person must be exonerated.

o Pardon

Each year before the end of term for the president of the United State, submitted to him is a list of names requesting pardon. It does not matter the crime whether it be minor or heinous, nor does it matter the sentencing long or short; what does matter is that the person receiving the pardon must be alive. God said that (Ezekiel 18:18 – 29) it does not matter what the person has done or how they lived their lives, if that person turn from his/her sins and ask for forgiveness and die the next day, he/she shall live because of his/her righteousness. But if a person lives that same length of time as a righteous person and then turn from righteousness to sin and die, that person shall die because of his/her sin. Therefore, the person must be alive in order to accept the pardon. Consider this **http://prideandprejudice86.spaces.live.com/Blog/ cns!37CF49520D7F9FF!130.entry. O. Henry (1862-1910)** was originally born William Sydney Porter in Greensboro, North

Carolina and was convicted of a capital offense in 1898. He was a noted author of many short stories, worked as a banker, and later learned the skill of embezzlement. He is convicted for embezzling about $785.00. After his death, attempts were made to get a pardon for O Henry but in order to get a pardon you must be alive to say, yes I will take it, or no I refuse it; he was already dead, therefore no action taken. The activity that gives a pardon value is acceptance. If a person refuses the pardon it is just worthless paper. Consider George Wilson convicted of robbing the US Mail and sentenced to die, receives a pardon from President Andrew Jackson. George Wilson refused the pardon and the case is elevated to the United States Supreme Court. After reviewing, the case The Court issues this statement as its finding.

- "A pardon is an act of grace, proceeding from the power entrusted with the execution of the laws, which exempts the individual, on whom it is bestowed, from the punishment the law inflicts for a crime he has committed...
- "A pardon is a deed, to the validity of which delivery is essential; and delivery is not completed without acceptance. It may then be rejected by the person to whom it is tendered; and if it be rejected, we have discovered no power in a court to force it on him.
- "It may be supposed that no being condemned to death would reject a pardon, but the rule must be the same in capital cases as in misdemeanors."

John Macpherson Berrien, Attorney-General said, "The court cannot give the prisoner the benefit of the pardon, unless he claims the benefit of it... It is a grant to him: it is his property; and he may accept it or not as he pleases."

Jesus has come to earth to pardon your sins and like George Wilson, it is your property, and you accept the free gift of life. But, if you refuse his pardon like George Wilson, you will reap the consequences. KJV Heb 3:7 [7] Wherefore (as the Holy Ghost saith, Today if ye will hear his voice, [8] Harden not your hearts, as in the provocation, in the day of temptation in the wilderness: George Wilson would not hear the voice of forgiveness and therefore perished. Jesus also validates the O Henry decision saying, "Seek me while I may be found, do not wait until it is too late." In these cases, for one the pardon is not accepted, and the other, the pardon came too late.

o   Acquittal

Before discussing acquittal it is necessary to paint a world view of its application to individuals, the laws governing and protecting society. In accordance with our criminal law codes, an innocent un-accused person does not need to be acquitted from anything. However, if that same person is indicted and prosecuted for an alleged offense, then the court must decide upon his/her innocence or guilt. If the judge rules that there is insufficient evidence to convict, or the jury finds the defendant not guilty, the person is acquitted. When God looks through the blood of Jesus and see you, will He say that there is insufficient evidence to convict you to hell. There are two kinds of acquittals, Acquittal "In Fact" and Acquittal " In Law." Each type does the job of removing all guilt from the person. Therefore, acquittal means that the person has been released from all the chains that binds them up.

In our Christian walk, we interchange the word acquittal with justification as being one and the same. Abraham, father of the Jewish nation receives justification or acquittal by putting his faith in God. Abraham believed God and is acquitted forever. In Romans 8:30 God has laid out a pronouncement of forgiveness to anyone repenting of their sin. The pronouncement from evil to good, from sin to righteousness is our justification. Because of our justification God has turned his wrath away from us and replaced it with continuous favor. In Psalm 32, King David expresses great joy and is glad for God to forgive him of sin. In justification God credits himself with the sin and bless David. We too are blessed and acquitted of all sin through the atoning blood of Jesus Christ.

o   Amnesty

Addressing the area of forgiveness known as amnesty, it is a vast subject and can be applied in many ways. When I first joined the military, I was sent to Fort Jackson South Carolina for training. One of the most important phases of training to me was hand to hand combat and at the rifle range firing the M16 A1 Rifle. During training on the rifle range we were issued live rounds (bullets) for target practice. After the training was over we picked up all of the spent shells and turned in all unfired (bullets) duds round. The drill sergeant marched us to the arms room to turn in the weapon and declared "NO BRASS – NO AMMO." When this phase was completed we returned to the barracks to retire for the day. However, before retiring from the day, the drill sergeant would always take us by the amnesty points. The amnesty points were the military way of giving you that one last chance to turn in all illegal items such as brass, ammo or anything unauthorized.

The unauthorized and or illegal activity haunting our lives is routed in sin. Jesus explains in His parable what we need amnesty from **Matthew 15:17-20 (KJV)** [17] Do not ye yet understand that whatsoever entereth in at the mouth goeth into the belly, and is cast out into the draught? [18] But those things which proceed out of the mouth come forth from the heart; and they defile the man. [19] For out of the heart proceed evil thoughts, murders, adulteries, fornications, thefts, false witness, and blasphemies: Jesus like the drill sergeant provides us with a second chance. He is the Amnesty relief point and forgiveness for all of our wrong and illegal activities. In Him all sin is justified. Yet amnesty reaches further than the individual level, it can wrap up the plea for mercy from war torn countries in captivity. These courtiers are in the same position as a sinner, wondering what I must do to be saved, and come on the Lord's side. Consider the jailer Paul talked about in the Book of Acts. **Acts 16:25-31 (KJV)** [25] And at midnight Paul and Silas prayed and sang praises unto God: and the prisoners heard them. [26] Suddenly there was a great earthquake, so that the foundations of the prison were shaken: and immediately all the doors were opened, and everyone's bands were loosed.

[27] And the keeper of the prison awaking out of his sleep, and seeing the prison doors open, he drew out his sword, and would have killed himself, supposing that the prisoners had been fled.

[28] But Paul cried with a loud voice, saying, Do thyself no harm: for we are all here. [29] Then he called for a light, and sprang in, and came trembling, and fell down before Paul and Silas,

[30] And brought them out, and said, Sirs, what must I do to be saved? [31] And they said, Believe on the Lord Jesus Christ, and thou shalt be saved, and thy house. Verse 31 is the kicker, **"Believe on the Lord Jesus Christ, and you will be saved, you and your household" (verse 31).** Believing on the Lord Jesus and making Him your master is all the amnesty needed to save not only you, but your household. Making Him your Lord and Master means that all of the other gods you are serving must be abandoned. The god of money (the love of money is different than the ownership of money), your beautiful home, that sports car or motorcycle you always wanted and now you have it, or your family. Love your family, but

know eternal soul. Believe on the one and only Son of God and amnesty is certain.

Do over or second chance

When I was about ten years old, growing up in a little place call Miccosukee Florida, we played marbles like today's children play video games. The rules of the game were simple but ridged enough to keep one's mind on the game continually. It went something like this. To start the game everyone would put one marble inside a circle (home) drawn on the ground. Then stand behind the home circle and toss the playing marble toward a long straight line called the toy. The person that was the closest to toy would (lag) first to home. Their goal was to hit the marble inside the ring and knock at least one marble out of the ring. If the marble came out of his hand wrong or someone got in the path between him and the home ring, he could ask for a do over. A do over was called slipper. God has given us that same opportunity in Jesus. When we were interacting and mingling with the wrong crowd, going off in the wrong direction Jesus steps in and gives us a second chance. Jesus gives us a second chance at life, a chance to get off of drugs and (for the older generations) alcohol and cigarettes. But our quality of life does not just lie in the material world; we must do the biding of the Father. Jesus said that He was required to do the work of He who had sent Him, and if we want to be like Jesus we must do the same. The first three people come to mind in the Bible that God has given a second chance is:

- *Hezekiah* – **Isaiah 38:1-6 (KJV)** [1] In those days was Hezekiah sick unto death. Isaiah the prophet the son of Amoz came unto him, and said unto him, Thus saith the LORD, Set thine house in order: for thou shalt die, and not live. [2] Then Hezekiah turned his face toward the wall, and prayed unto the LORD, [3] And said, Remember now, O LORD, I beseech thee, how I have walked before thee in truth and with a perfect heart, and have done *that which is* good in thy sight, and Hezekiah wept sore. [4] Then came the word of the LORD to Isaiah, saying, [5] Go, and say to Hezekiah, Thus saith the LORD, the God of David thy father, I have heard thy prayer, I have seen thy tears: behold, I will add unto thy days fifteen years. [6] And I will deliver thee and this city out of the hand of the king of Assyria: and I will defend this city.

- *Joana* – **Jonah 2:1-2 (KJV)** [1] Then Jonah prayed unto the LORD his God out of the fish's belly, [2] And said, I cried by reason of mine affliction unto the LORD, and he heard me; out of the belly of hell cried I, *and* thou heardest my voice. **Jonah 2:10 (KJV)** [10] And the LORD spake unto the fish, and it vomited out Jonah upon the dry *land.* **Jonah 3:1-3 (KJV)** [1] And the word of the LORD came unto Jonah the second time, saying, [2] Arise, go unto Nineveh, that great city, and preach unto it the preaching that I bid thee. [3] So Jonah arose, and went unto Nineveh, according to the word of the LORD. Now Nineveh was an exceeding great city of three days' journey.

- *Paul* – **Acts 9:10-18 (KJV)** [10] And there was a certain disciple at Damascus, named Ananias; and to him said the Lord in a vision, Ananias. And he said, Behold, I *am here*, Lord. [11] And the Lord *said* unto him, Arise, and go into the street which is called Straight, and enquire in the house of Judas for *one* called Saul, of Tarsus: for, behold, he prayeth, [12] And hath seen in a vision a man named Ananias coming in and putting *his* hand on him, that he might receive his sight. [13] Then Ananias answered, Lord, I have heard by many of this man, how much evil he hath done to thy saints at Jerusalem: [14] And here he hath authority from the chief priests to bind all that call on thy name.

[15] But the Lord said unto him, Go thy way: for he is a chosen vessel unto me, to bear my name before the Gentiles, and kings, and the children of Israel:

[16] For I will shew him how great things he must suffer for my name's sake. [17] And Ananias went his way, and entered into the house; and putting his hands on him said, Brother Saul, the Lord, *even* Jesus, that appeared unto thee in the way as thou camest, hath sent me, that thou mightest receive thy sight, and be filled with the Holy Ghost.

[18] And immediately there fell from his eyes as it had been scales: and he received sight forthwith, arose, and was baptized.

These are but a few of the examples of how God is the God of second chances. These men portrayed are extreme examples, and if God is willing to let them have a do over, you've got one coming too.

Reprieve

When all else fails and it seems that we are doomed to face the consequences of our action, a reprieve is necessary to stay the hand from our punishment. The reprieve postpones the allotted or prescribed penalty. The first person needing a reprieve was Adam; Adam was told by God in plain easy to follow instructions. Adam's instruction was this, (eat of every tree of the Garden except of the tree of the knowledge of good and evil. **Genesis 2:16-17 (KJV)**. After partaking of the tree in the mist of the garden, Adam's eyes were opened and he was aware of another side of life, sin and evil. Because of his new found knowledge he is also conscious of the fact that he has disobeyed God. Adam begins to follow rules that would be written thousands of years after his time. These rules are called the Hierarchy of Needs written by Abraham Maslow in his 1943 paper, "A Theory of Human Motivation." After he committed the infraction and eats from the tree of good and evil, he feels that divine separation from God and the world. Upon God's next visit, Adam takes matters into his own hands to handle sin, by covering it up. God quickly assigned sentence to Adam for his sin and expels him from the garden. God does this because of His love for mankind. At the time, it may have seemed like punishment to Adam, but now we the Monday Night Quarterbacks can clearly see that this next statement is a reprieve. **Genesis 3:22 (KJV)** [22] And the LORD God said, Behold, the man is become as one of us, to know good and evil: and now, lest he put forth his hand, and take also of the tree of life, and eat, and live forever:

At this point you may ask yourself, how in the world is getting kicked of the garden and not being allowed to eat from the tree of life anything except punishment. First of all, we know that God's love for us is genuine and not filled with conditional disillusion and disappointment. Satan disappointed all of the people in the world at one time, and as quickly as a short lived vapor, he deserts them as well. But God is forever faithful in His relationship with us to supply all of our needs according to His riches in glory. Adam and Eve were bound in sin; and in the book of James we find that the end of sin is death. Without a savior, man is doomed to die separate and apart from God. God's first act of salvation is to spare mankind from God's ultimate punishment "Eternal damnation." If Adam was allowed to partake of the tree of life; he would live forever, forever in sin. Because forever points to the very end, mankind would have no chance for penitence. But God was merciful enough to shield Adam from the tree of life in order to stop him from committing an even worse act. Eating of the tree of life gave life, and in the case of Adam, it would be giving continuous existence to sin. But God saves us from ourselves so that we may find rest and salvation in Jesus.

- Clemency

We as humans need rest for our evil deeds, and clemency or mercy to postpone the inevitable fate that lies ahead of us. As Christians we study and examine the question of mercy in many ways. Some of our evaluations are rigid and militaristic. We see the person not as an advocate to provide clemency, but a sinner on the wrong side of the Gospel; because we have been trained to view mercy as being too soft or promiscuous. But dear friends, never forget that Jesus is in position to make that same type of Judgment concerning you, instead He grants clemency. You must do the same, but with wisdom. As Christians, we are to copy the patterns of Jesus and turn from the world's view. The world does not grant clemency for wrongful or criminal acts against a person. However, we must; but we also have the responsibility to guard our affairs with great care. **Matthew 10:16 (KJV)** [16] Behold, I send you forth as sheep in the midst of wolves: be ye therefore wise as serpents, and harmless as doves. However, the most important features of forgiveness are its capacity for leniency, pity, compassion and kindness.

Unforgiveness

What does it take for you to be able to forgive someone? It may seem like an easy task, but to some it is harder than manual labor. We often associate unforgiveness with acts that a person or persons have done against us. However it runs deeper and produce the fruits of evil; like bitterness, malice, pride, revenge, and vanity. Satan wants unforgiveness in your heart, and it does not matter to him how or why it is there. For example; Satan has effectively used the media to turn O. J. Simpson into one of the most hated men in America. Millions of people hold bitterness in their hearts for O. J. because of the outcome of his trial. He was accused of brutally slaying two people, his ex-wife Nicole Brown-Simpson, and Ronald Goldman in 1994. In 1995 O. J. Simpson put together a dream team defense system of attorneys, and was acquitted of the slayings. However, America and the media had a different vote, "guilty." The people provided the paint and the media tagged O. J. with bright red labels that read "MURDERER." When bitterness last over-time, it turns into a grudge awaiting revenge. Well, time has passed and the eagerly awaiting public has finally carved their name in O. J.'s hide. Under what some would consider trumped up charges, O. J. will now spend 30++ years in prison. Judge Jackie Glass does not break in sentencing and afterward one of the jurors makes this comment. He finally got what he deserves. The question almost begs itself; was O. J.'s verdict and sentencing the product of malice and revenge?

We have all been in one way or the other upset, wounded or hurt by people in our lives and forgiveness may not seem like the correct course of action, but it is. Paul says in the book of Ephesians that if we are not able to forgive a person, then allow that person to obtain forgiveness through the God in us. We must put aside every weight that so easily beset us and allow God to handle all our retaliations. God handles our small and large hurtles with life in the person of Jesus Christ to keep us out of harm's way. Because unforgiveness is continuous willful, sin- filled with anger and hostility, therefore, Jesus shows us the pattern and importance of unforgiveness in the Lord's Prayer (KJV Matt 6: 14–15). In addition He (Jesus) tells Peter that (Matt 18:21–22) that a person must forgive another 70 times 7. Meaning that the person would lose count somewhere on the way to 490 times and forget about the whole matter.

Does unforgiveness affect our lives and happiness? Before answering this question, remember the example (pg 92) about missionary and her family situation. The bitterness directed toward her opened a 12 year gap in their lives. A gap is equivalent to a void, and a void must be filled with something. The something that Satan filled the gap with is (1) relational problems (your bitterness will carry over into other relationships), (2) Physical and Emotional Problems (mental health issues, stress related illnesses, and high blood pressure just to name a few), and (3) Our relationship with God. James says that the effectual fervent prayers of the righteous availeth much, therefore we must strive to overcome unforgiveness.

How do we overcome unforgiveness? **Matthew 5:23-24 (KJV)**

²³ Therefore if thou bring thy gift to the altar, and there rememberest that thy brother hath ought against thee;

²⁴ Leave there thy gift before the altar, and go thy way; first be reconciled to thy brother, and then come and offer thy gift. If unforgiveness toward a person is in your heart, then it can affect the quality of your spiritual life as well. Jesus says, get it out in the open, then come and commune with Him. Sometimes it is not easy to approach a person concerning forgiveness. In times like this, surrender it all to Jesus, because Jesus and Jesus alone is the only one that can help you. When God is in control, all we have to do is forget about whatever it was that was bothering us, right!

Whereas putting God in control of your anger, and other factors keeping you from being able to forgive someone is an important first step, all is not over. We often here the adage "if you have truly forgiven a person, then you will forget it." This statement also implies that you are now able to become friends again as though nothing ever happened. Is this true? According to my account of how the body functions, it is physically impossible to forget anything. However, you may reconcile your differences and live in harmony, and according to the seriousness of the tort time will heal your heart. Once time has run its course the negative ties that binds you to your own little world, will be unlocked by the keys of forgiveness. Forgiveness of sin is the reason for the coming of Jesus.

CHAPTER 8

The Coming of Jesus

—ɯ—

Introduction

The book of Matthew is my personal preference and will be used to discuss activities surrounding the birth, ministry, death and resurrection of our Lord and Savior Jesus Christ. My reason preference points this way because, Matthew begins his account of Jesus by listing a long string of names that makes you want to just skip on to the next chapter or close the book altogether. I know what you are thinking and you are not alone, you are thinking why doesn't he just put this list in an appendix and get on with the story. Well, Matthew was a Jew, and to a Jew the lineage of an individual was a compelling slice of information that must be included when telling the story of a person's life. The natural writing style of the Hebrews was to prove the pedigree before the historian penned the autobiography. The reason pedigree was so important goes back to the book of Exodus and surfaces again in the book of Ezra; it was to prove purity of lineage, and rights to belong. If even the most minute tainting or mixture of blood could be found throughout the lineage of a person, that person was not considered a Jew and did not have the right to be a member of the people of God.

Ezra 2:60-63 (KJV) ⁶⁰ The children of Delailah, the children of Tobiah, the children of Nekoda, six hundred fifty and two. [61] And of the children of the priests: the children of Habaiah, the children of Koz, the children of Barzillai; which took a wife of the daughters of Barzillai the Gileadite, and was called after their name: [62] These sought their register *among* those that were reckoned by genealogy, but they were not found: therefore were they, as polluted, put from the Priesthood. [63] And the Tirshatha said unto them, that they should not eat of the most holy things, till there stood up a Priest with Urim and with Thummim. Ezra did consider these Priests. **http://latter-rain.com/ltrain/herodg.htm** King Herod the Great is another example of purity in lineage in question. Pureblooded Jews hated him because His mother Kypros was an Arab, his father Antipater an Idumaean therefore he was half Edomite. Was this important to Herod, you bet, so much so that he destroys all of the original records in an effort to hide the fact that he was not a pure Jew.

Matthew thinks that lineage should be important to us also; therefore, he arranges the names in mnemonic order. He does this because at the times of his writing, books were rare, and only the very rich could afford a written book, other had to committee them to memory. The mnemonic order Matthew arranges the lineage of Jesus in is three groups, each group having fourteen generations. Matthew chooses this order for another important reason, because it shows the historical progression of the Jewish nation from Abraham until the coming of Christ. The first phase or order ends the fourteen-generation and the accomplishments with David, King of Israel. King David was God's choice as Israel first King, however Saul was the people's choice therefore Samuel anoints Saul King for the people, but David was God's anointed. David called the man after his own heart is his King over Israel. Under the leadership of David, Israel becomes a nation. Phase 2 covers the period of Israel's disobedience and shame, and the punishment resulting from their actions. Israel behaved badly; they worshipped idol gods, would not listen to the Prophets, and treated one another evil, therefore, God allowed them to be overpowered and taken into exile in Babylon. Phase 3 marks the coming of Jesus, the redeemer of our sins and bondage. In summation, the three stages show the spiritual growth of Israel and that the Law although perfect in every way, was not the answer to our salvation. Jesus is the answer.

Genealogy

Let us take a further look at the way Matthew lays out Chapter 1:1–17 and strap it to Genesis Chapter 1:26. Just as God makes David King in phase 1 of the lineage of Jesus, He does the same for man in phase 1 of the creation. However, God takes it a step further in that He not only makes man King of the world and His relatives; man has supreme authority (not gender bias). **Genesis 1:26 (KJV)** [26] And God said, "Let us make man in our image, after our likeness: and let them have dominion over the fish of the sea, and over the fowl of the air, and over the cattle, and over all the earth, and over every creeping thing that creepeth upon the earth." Man made in the image of God, but would soon lose that image to sin. Sin brings up the second phase of man, which makes him subject to his own devices. God corrects and puts Israel on the straight path again, but they did not follow totally after God; therefore, they needed an intercessor to plead their cause. The intercessor pleading their cause brings us down to the last phase, "Jesus."

Thus far we have addressed the issues as they apply to the house of Jacob or Israel, and hinted slightly toward Jesus. However, this section will deal primarily with the analysis of the lineage and each stage thereof. First things first, the genealogy chart prove that Jesus is royalty and meets the criteria of being of the house of David as fore told by the Prophets of the Old Testament. In Matthew Chapter 22, Jesus asks the Jews this question; **Matthew 22:42 (KJV)** [42] Saying, "What think ye of Christ? whose son is he?" They say unto him, *The Son* of David. Proof again that Jesus is the Lord and righteous one to come as the messiah with all power in heaven and on earth. Matthew's genealogy shows us the kingdom of God and Jesus as the legal King foretold in Isaiah chapter 7 **Isaiah 7:13-14 (KJV)** [13] And he said, "Hear ye now, O house of David; *Is it* a small thing for you to weary men, but will ye weary my God also?" [14] Therefore the Lord himself shall give you a sign; Behold, a virgin shall conceive, and bear a son, and shall call his name Immanuel.

Take a look at the criteria wrapped inside these two verses, Jesus must be of the house of David via both the mother and father, and borne to a virgin. He does meet the qualifications in that both Mary and Joseph; his earthly parent's roots are traceable to King David. This genealogy chart of Matthew shows how the grace of God abounds to all, he includes the names of four women in the lineup. This stretch has strained the imagination of every red blood Jew, because women were possessions or things, and usually not mentioned in the main stream of business. In fact, one of the morning prayers of a Jewish man was: 'Lord, I thank You that You haven't made me a Gentile, You haven't made me a slave, and You haven't made me a woman'

The Birth of Jesus

Matthew 1:18-25 (KJV) [18] Now the birth of Jesus Christ was on this wise: When as his mother Mary was espoused to Joseph, before they came together, she was found with child of the Holy Ghost. This passage of verse is installed immediately as proof that Joseph could not possibly be the natural father of Jesus. Mary was espoused to Joseph, meaning that they were engaged or betrothal. During the betrothal period, there is no physical contact like sex; however, the relationship is binding. Betrothal is a vow taken between the couples and God to maintain purity in their relationship to each other, until consummation. Some betrothal period went on for years, nevertheless the commitment was binding; the couples could not end the engagement without a writing of divorcement. Joseph knew that the child Jesus was not his natural son, and could have opted out of the union.

[19] Then Joseph her husband, being a just *man*, and not willing to make her a public example, was minded to put her away privily. [20] But while he thought on these things, behold, the angel of the Lord appeared unto him in a dream, saying, Joseph, thou son of David, fear not to take unto thee Mary thy wife: for that which is conceived in her is of the Holy Ghost. Why would Joseph want out, did he believe that she was unfaithful to him? My answer is a qualified "yes" yes because of verse 20. Verse 20 says while he thought on these things: indicating that Mary's condition was constantly on his mind, and not favorable. Verse 19 again the indication is that he believes that she was unfaithful, because he wants to put her away. However, he did not want to make a public example out of her, but minded to divorce her privately. Why put her away privately? There were at least two reasons for not making a public example of her, (1) because of the law of betroth and the remedies prescribed by this law. Under the conditions as set forth in Deuteronomy 22, Mary was a true candidate for stoning, and in-accordance with the Jewish customs Joseph would have to cast the first stone.

Deuteronomy 22:23-24 (KJV)[23] If a damsel *that is* a virgin be betrothed unto an husband, and a man find her in the city, and lie with her; [24] Then ye shall bring them both out unto the gate of that city, and ye shall stone them with stones that they die; the damsel, because she cried not, *being* in the city; and the man, because he hath humbled his neighbor's wife: so thou shalt put away evil from among you,

(2) Because of Law of Jealousy. Acts of defilement such as unfaithfulness between betrothal partners was as much the public ceremony as for a couple that has been married for years. The jealous husband's suspicions were publically carried out by the office of the Priest at the door of the tabernacle. Everyone from the camp could attend, making his private business a public matter. Consider this, a public exposure of his marital problems brought to the fore front hidden traits of his character. They would think to themselves, since no one has ever used this option; he did not love and only wanted to hurt her. But what if he was wrong, would the relationship ever return to normal. It may, but it would require work and time.

Numbers 5:11-30 (KJV) [14] And the spirit of jealousy come upon him, and he being jealous of his wife, and she being defiled: or if the spirit of jealousy come upon him, and he be jealous of his wife, and she be not defiled: [15] Then shall the man bring his wife unto the Priest, and he shall bring her offering for her, the tenth *part* of an ephah of barley meal; he shall pour no oil upon it, nor put frankincense thereon; for it *is* an offering of jealousy, an offering of memorial, bringing iniquity to remembrance.

[21] And she shall bring forth a son, and thou shalt call his name JESUS: for he shall save his people from their sins. [22] Now all this was done, that it might be fulfilled which was spoken of the Lord by the prophet, saying, [23] Behold, a virgin shall be with child, and shall bring forth a son, and they shall call his name Emmanuel, which being interpreted is, God with us. [24] Then Joseph being raised from sleep did as the angel of the Lord had bidden him, and took unto him his wife: [25] And knew her not till she had brought forth her first-born son: and he called his name JESUS.

This segment of scripture from verse 21 through 25 shows the other nature of Jesus, His human side. It is confirmed that He was both fully human via the birth of Mary and fully God via the implantation of the Holy Spirit. The Prophet Isaiah's prophesy concerning the birth of Jesus to a virgin fulfilled. **Isaiah 7:13-14 (KJV)** [13] And he said, Hear ye now, O house of David; *Is it* a small thing for you to weary men, but will ye weary my God also?

[14] Therefore the Lord himself shall give you a sign; Behold, a virgin shall conceive, and bear a son, and shall call his name Immanuel. The name Jesus is the Greek translation for the Hebrew word Joshua, which means Jehovah is salvation (Barclay, pp19). Just as Joshua took over as leader of the Exodus to Canaan, Jesus (Joshua) has taken over as captain and High Priest who constantly makes intersession for our souls.

In Isaiah chapter 7:1–14 God tries to reach the self-righteous King Ahaz with information about the coming of Jesus. When King Ahaz refuses the sign, God makes the sign universally known to the entire house of David, that sign is the birth of God in the flesh (Isaiah 7:14) via a virgin mother. What is a virgin mother? During the times of ancient Israel, the parents or someone who were professional matchmakers did marriage (Barclay, pp18–19); the agreement between the two families finalized the engagement. The engagement could go on for years, however when the female becomes of age she has the choice to opt out of the relationship, if she does not then they are locked in the betrothal phase. During the betrothal, the couples were married, but put on hold for a one-year period. Afterward, the marriage is proper through marriage rituals. The thing that puzzles the Jews was this; the Bible only list four ways for a person to come into the world. (1) Genesis 1:26–28 God formed man out of the dust of the ground. (2) Genesis 2:21–23 God made eve from a rib in Adam's side. (3) Man has relationship with woman (biological parents). (4) The Holy Spirits impregnates the mother of Jesus, a biological mother and supernatural father (Luke 1). The Genealogy Chart of Jesus

The book of the generation of Jesus Christ, the son of David, the son of Abraham

from Abraham to David *are* fourteen generations	1. 1 Abraham begat Isaac	**Birth of Isaac**
	2. 2 Isaac begat Jacob;	**Genesis 21:1-8 (KJV)**
	3. 3 Jacob begat Judas his brethren;	[1] And the LORD visited Sarah as he had said, and the LORD did unto Sarah as he had spoken.
	4. 4 Judas begat Phares	
	Zara of Thamar;	[2] For Sarah conceived, and bare Abraham a son in his old age, at the set time of which God had spoken to him.
	5. 5 Phares begat Esrom;	
	6. **6Esrom** begat Aram;	[3] And Abraham called the name of his son that was born unto him, whom Sarah bare to him, Isaac.
	7. **7 Aram** begat Aminadab;	
	8. **8 Aminadab** begat Naasson;	
	9. **9 Naasson** begat Salmon;	
	10. **10 Salmon** begat Booz of Rachab;	

	11. **11 Booz** begat Obed of Ruth;	**David Made King** **2 Samuel 5:3-5 (KJV)** ³ So all the elders of Israel came to the king to Hebron; and king David made a league with them in Hebron before the LORD: and they anointed David king over Israel. ⁴ David *was* thirty years old when he began to reign, *and* he reigned forty years. ⁵ In Hebron he reigned over Judah seven years and six months: and in Jerusalem he reigned thirty and three years over all Israel and Judah.
	12. 12 **Obed** begat Jesse; ⁶ And 13. **13 Jesse** begat David the king 14. **14 David** the king begat Solomon of her that had been the wife of Urias;	

David until the carrying away into Babylon *are* fourteen generations;	15. **15 Solomon** begat Roboam; 16. **16 Roboam** begat Abia; 17. 17 **Abia** begat Asa; 18. 18 **Asa** begat Josaphat; 19. 19 **Josaphat** begat Joram; 20. **20 Joram** begat Ozias; 21. 21 **Ozias** begat Joatham; 22. **22 Joatham** begat Achaz; 23. 23 **Achaz** begat Ezekias; 24. **24 Ezekias** begat Manasses; 25. **25 Manasses** begat Amon; 26. 26 **Amon** begat Josias; 27. 27 <u>**Josias** begat Jechonias and his brethren, about the time they were carried away</u>	**Carrying Away Into Babylon** **2 Kings 24:13-14 (KJV)** [14] And he carried away all Jerusalem, and all the princes, and all the mighty men of valour, *even* ten thousand captives, and all the craftsmen and smiths: none remained, save the poorest sort of the people of the land. --- **Jeremiah 27:21-22 (KJV)** [21] Yea, thus saith the LORD of hosts, the God of Israel, concerning the vessels that remain *in* the house of the LORD, and *in* the house of the king of Judah and of Jerusalem; [22] They shall be carried to Babylon, and there shall they be until the day that I visit them, saith the LORD; then will I

	to Babylon: after they were brought to Babylon,	bring them up, and restore them to this place.
	28. **28 Jechonias** begat Salathiel;	
	29. **29 Salathiel** begat Zorobabel;	
from the carrying away into Babylon unto Christ *are* fourteen generations.	30. **30 Zorobabel** begat Abiud;	
	31. **31 Abiud** begat Eliakim;	
	32. **32 Eliakim** begat Azor;	
	33. **33 Azor** begat Sadoc;	
	34. **34 Sadoc** begat Achim;	
	35. **35 Achim** begat Eliud;	
	36. **36 Eliud** begat Eleazar;	
	37. **37 Eleazar** begat Matthan;	
	38. **38 Matthan** begat Jacob;	
	39. **39 Jacob** begat Joseph	

	40. **40 Joseph** husband of Mary, of whom was born Jesus, who is called Christ.	

(all information contained herein the chart above is taken directly from the King James Version of the Bible.)

Visit of the wise men

This chapter is broken into two segments, first the birthplace of Jesus and His visitation from the wise men, and second flight to Egypt, God's intervention for the safety of baby Jesus and his family, and the fulfillment of prophesy.

The setting for the birthplace of Jesus is a little town about six miles outside of Jerusalem called Bethlehem (Ephrath). Bethlehem was as the song goes, high and lifted up, some two thousand five hundred feet high waiting to provide the world with a piece of history that would live forever. This history begins in Genesis with Jacob memorializing the grave of Rachel **(Genesis 35:20 48:7)**. It was in this same city where Ruth married Boaz and becomes one of the ancestors of Jesus. It was in this city where the apple of God's eye (King David) when hunted as a rebel, longed for a drink of water from its well. Finally but not all-inclusive, it is the place foretold by the prophet Micah to be the birthplace of Jesus. **Micah 5:2 (KJV)** [2] But thou, Bethlehem Ephratah, *though* thou be little among the thousands of Judah, *yet* out of thee shall he come forth unto me *that is* to be ruler in Israel; whose goings forth *have been* from of old, from everlasting. However, in the prospectus of Matthew Chapter 2:1 – 12, it was a place of worship.

Last Sunday (Nov 30, 2008) the pastor (Bishop Kimble) discussed praise and worship in almost opposite terms than the way we are presently doing it. He goes on to say that the songs and hymns used to put us in that just right mood to receive the presence of God is ok, but should not be an end within themselves. True worship is as described in Matthew about the wise men or Magi. They saw the star and searched for the place of Jesus' birth, traveling as much as 700 miles. When they found the baby Jesus, their mission was to render the respect of royalty to Him with gifts that only the children of Kings received. After the royal welcoming ceremony is over, the Magi returns to their country as suddenly as they had come. God knowing the heart of King Herod warns Joseph to flee into Egypt, because "The House of Bread" soon becomes spoiled, and full of molded.

Matthew 2:1-12 (KJV) [1] Now when Jesus was born in Bethlehem of Judaea in the days of Herod the king, behold, there came wise men from the east to Jerusalem,

Born in Bethlehem

Jesus was born in the town of Bethlehem. There are two towns by that name appearing in the bible, Bethlehem-Judah a tiny Village elevated high in the mountains just outside of Jerusalem, and Bethlehem-Zebulun the inheritance of Zebulun which contained twelve cities with their villages **(Josh 19:15)**. Bethlehem-Judah is our focus, the place formally known as Ephrath where Rachel gave birth to Benjamin and dies **(Gen 35:19)**, where Elimelech the Bethlehemite takes Naomi to Moab then later dies leaving Orpah and Ruth as Naomi's dependents. Orpah goes back to her people, while Ruth stays with Naomi and return to Ephrath (Bethlehem-Judah). Then history is in the making, Ruth marries Boaz and gives birth to Obed the father of Jesse, the father of King David.

It is this place of which Micah speaks these words **Micah 5:2 (KJV)** But thou, Bethlehem Ephratah, *though* thou be little among the thousands of Judah, *yet* out of thee shall he come forth unto me *that is* to be ruler in Israel; whose goings forth *have been* from of old, from everlasting. Later in history **Luke 2:4 – 7 (KJV)** — And Joseph also went up from Galilee, out of the city of Nazareth, into Judaea, unto the city of David, which is called Bethlehem; (because he was of the house and lineage of David:) [5] To be taxed with Mary his espoused wife, being great with child. [6] And so it was, that, while they were there, the days were accomplished that she should be delivered. [7] And she brought forth her firstborn son, and wrapped him in swaddling clothes, and laid him in a manger; because there was no room for them in the inn.

Herod the king

Antipas	
Antipater	

Antipater	
	Sons:
	Joseph
	Pheroras
	Phasaelus
Herod [1] +Cleopatra	Herod Philip [8] + Salome*[6]
Herod[1]+Malthake	Archelaus [2]
	Olympias
	Herod-Antipas [4] +Herodias*[5]
	Son:
	Herod
	Agrippa
	Aristobulus
Herod[1]+Mariamne	Herod Philip [3] +Herodias [5]
Herod[1]+**Mariamne-II**	
	Philip [3] +Herodias [5]

Costobarus + Salome
   Children:
Alexander   **Aristobulus**+Berenice
Cypros   Aristobulus
Salampsio   Herodias [5]
                        Herod-Agrippa[7]
                        Agrippa [9]
                        Bernice [10]

Children

Mariamne
Drusilla
Drusus

Born in (73-4 BCE) the Idumean decent King Herod came into power because of the Roman exertion of power over the weakening Hasmonean. Although this dismal period of Roman authority under Julius Cesar restricts the Jewish leaders to Judea, it does serve to improve tension in the area. It is during this period that Herod gains the trust of the Roman Government and the Roman Government post him as King of Judea. As King, Herod starts out in the right direction; he is concerned about his people. On several occasions, he waves or reduces taxes during times of depression. During the times of famine, he gives out of his private treasure to feed starving people. However, this would soon end because; King Herod had one fatal moral deficiency. He was overly suspicious. Moreover, the older he got the more suspicious he becomes. His suspicion caused him to kill anyone that he thought was trying to take over his position. He not only eliminated political rivals, he killed his own family (see lineage chart above, marked in **BOLD** these are family members killed by King Herod) . After the death of

King Herod, the Kingdom divides into three regions, with his heirs Archelaus, Antipas the tetrarch and Philip as the leadership or Kings over each of the regions.

[2] Saying, Where is he that is born King of the Jews? For we have seen his star in the east, and are come to worship him. The people we know and call the wise men were more than just a pool of shepherds sitting on some soft rock somewhere in a desert pasture caring for a flock of sheep. Herodotus of Halicarnassus the Greek historian who lived during 5th century BC (484 BC – 425 BC) records much of the long and winding turns in their history. He calls them the Magi and tracks their origin to Median. The Medes was one of the Persian Empires that attempted and failed to overthrow Persia. After failing to overthrow Persia, they resolved to become a tribe of Priests. They were the Persian equivalent of Israel's Levites. They were the Priests in charge of all religious functions, rituals, sacrifices, traditions, medicine, magic, and natural science. These group of people, although elevated by the Persian as their Levites were anything but Levites. Even though they searched for truth and were honest in their finding, they were in our modern day terms, Simon the great one of Samaria (Acts 8:9–11) or "Elymas the Sorcerer" (Acts 13:6–8) (Elymas is a Arabic word meaning wise). These wise men chief information came from gazing into the skies at the stars "Astrology" looking for the unveiling of knowledge. This time knowledge accomplished was by the voice of wisdom directing them to follow the sign and pay homage to our savior. Receiving homage from other countries is one of the prerequisites of a King, the wise men satisfy this requirement. [3] When Herod the king had heard *these things*, he was troubled, and all Jerusalem with him. [4] And when he had gathered all the Chief Priests and Scribes of the people together, he demanded of them where Christ should be born. In this occasion Herod the King is symbolically used as a living power point showing people in great

authority as Jesus' most powerful enemy. Because murder was as second nature to him as eating or drinking, the people of Jerusalem feared. They knew what Herod was capable of and immediately Herod confirmed their worst superstitions. He campaigned the death of Jesus on a massive scale. First He collects data as to when and where the child will be born, as operation plan B. [5] And they said unto him, In Bethlehem of Judaea: for thus it is written by the prophet, [6] And thou Bethlehem, *in* the land of Juda, art not the least among the princes of Juda: for out of thee shall come a Governor, that shall rule my people Israel. Herod collects this information from his most creditable sources, the people who know and live the Old Testament Scriptures, the Priests. The Scripture read to him was from Mica 5:2, showing Jesus as the person to shepherd Israel into a new era; the era of salvation. Then he formats his plan of attack, first to get the wise men to tell him where they last seen the baby Jesus. [7] Then Herod, when he had privily called the wise men, enquired of them diligently what time the star appeared. [8] And he sent them to Bethlehem, and said, Go and search diligently for the young child; and when ye have found *him*, bring me word again, that I may come and worship him also. [9] When they had heard the king, they departed; and, lo, the star, which they saw in the east, went before them, till it came and stood over where the young child was. [10] When they saw the star, they rejoiced with exceeding great joy. [11] And when they were come into the house, they saw the young child with Mary his mother, and fell down, and worshipped him: and when they had opened their treasures, they presented unto him gifts; gold, and frankincense, and myrrh

Warning of God

Flight to Egypt

[12] And being warned of God in a dream that they should not return to Herod, they departed into their own country another way. **Matthew 2:13-18 (KJV)** [13] And when they were departed, behold, the angel of the Lord appeareth to Joseph in a dream, saying, Arise, and take the young child and his mother, and flee into Egypt, and be thou there until I bring thee word: for Herod will seek the young child to destroy him. [14] When he arose, he took the young child and his mother by night, and departed into Egypt: [15] And was there until the death of Herod: that it might be fulfilled which was spoken of the Lord by the Prophet, "Saying, Out of Egypt have I called my son." [16] Then Herod, when he saw that he was mocked of the wise men, was exceeding wroth, and sent forth, and slew all the children that were in Bethlehem, and in all the coasts thereof, from two years old and under, according to the time which he had diligently enquired of the wise men. [17] Then was fulfilled that which was spoken by Jeremy the prophet, saying, [18] In Rama was there a voice heard, lamentation, and weeping, and great mourning, Rachel weeping *for* her children, and would not be comforted, because they are not.

As we can see by verse 12-18 that plan A does not work, so therefore Herod executes plan B. Plan B was the shock and awe of that period. He commands his chief thugs to search out the area and kill that baby. However, because they did not know who the baby Jesus was, all babies born during that time period was to be executed. I have heard pastors paint the picture of thousands of babies being killed, but history records only approximately twenty to thirty babies killed. One is too many. God knows the hearts and minds of everyone and therefore, He warns Joseph to leave the area and go to Egypt. It took courage for Joseph to take up and leave his well known homeland. He would not be alone in Egypt because it was populated with Jewish segments numbering over one million people.

Joseph obeys and heeds the warning. He takes his family and begins the move; however during his flight to Egypt obstacles come up that seemingly would require negotiation, but God was with Jesus, and Jesus was with the family. Legend has it that on the way to Egypt Joseph's family comes under attack by Villains wanting to take what little goods they had. However, the person (Dismas) leading the band of robbers was himself a misfit, throw back Jew. He was born on the wrong side of the tracks, in the worst possible time for Jews. They were the bottom climbing up toward pond scum. His parents were poor and therefore could not afford a Gamaliel for him to learn from. His trade in life was learned on the streets in and around Jerusalem, how to cheat, rob and steal. He was street wise and formed a band of thieves like himself to partner with. While in route to Egypt his band of thieves lay wait and traps Joseph and his family for the purpose to rob them. Dismas later known as (Saint Dimas) comes upon the family with the **http://en.wikipedia.org/wiki/Good_Thief#.22Dismas.3F.22** intent to do harm and then takes one look at the baby Jesus. Instantly he realizes that this is a special baby and believed that the baby knew and could understand him. He holds back the band of robbers, and turns back to Jesus a second time, uttering these words. I know that you are special, and if the time ever comes that you can do a favor for me; forget not thou this hour. Then he escorts Joseph and Mary to the border of Egypt and returns to his old ways. Thirty three years later his luck would run out. It seemed that this time he was at the wrong place at the wrong time, because he is caught and his life would end in shame on a Roman Cross. But hanging beside him was Jesus who fulfills the promise to do a favor for him in his time of need. Jesus does the only favor that he will ever need. "This day you shall be with me in paradise."

Call out of Egypt

Matthew 2:19-23 (KJV) [19] But when Herod was dead, behold, an angel of the Lord appeareth in a dream to Joseph in Egypt, [20] Saying, Arise, and take the young child and his mother, and go into the land of Israel: for they are dead which sought the young child's life. [21] And he arose, and took the young child and his mother, and came into the land of Israel. [22] But when he heard that Archelaus did reign in Judaea in the room of his father Herod, he was afraid to go thither: notwithstanding, being warned of God in a dream, he turned aside into the parts of Galilee: [23] And he came and dwelt in a city called Nazareth: that it might be fulfilled which was spoken by the prophets, He shall be called a Nazarene.

Although Herod was dead, his murdering spirit is alive and well in King Archelaus. Archelaus, is As Rehoboam 1 Kings 12:12 (ESV) he would rule with a fist of iron, and be as a scorpion; his little finger would be thicker than the loins of his father King Herod the Great. His father murdered a great many people, but nothing compared to this man. His first targets were the Sanhedrin Counsel. Some three thousand people murdered. This was an evil King, therefore God warns Joseph again to turn aside from Juda and go into Galilee.

The Kingdom of Heaven

Jesus Silent Years

Before we look at John the Baptist and his ministry, it may do us well to take a quick peek at the end of Matthew's accounts in chapter two and the beginning of chapter three. At the end of chapter two Jesus is a child, and before you can wink your eye, chapter three begins with Jesus as a full grown man of thirty years old with Him filing form 1040 as Head of Household. Do you ever wonder what went on between the end of chapter two and beginning of chapter three? Well wonder no longer.

start here Jesus the first the only begotten Son of God, was also the first born of Joseph and Mary. He was the Immaculate Conception, born to a virgin mother. And because He fits the categories of being first born fully God and first born fully human, He had the human responsibility to continue the strength of Joseph (Deuteronomy 21:17). This continuation is known as rights of first born and birth rights. Although these rights may sometimes be used interchangeably they are different. To explain the difference between the blessing of the first born and a birth right, I will treat the birthright first then move on to the blessing of firstborn in the interest of flow.

Birthrights

Birthright is an inheritance usually given to the oldest male child as a means of sustaining the family after the death of the father. The oldest child would receive what is known as a double portion of the father's estate while the others would receive only a single portion. A double portion because now he would become head of household and have the responsibility to take care of his mother, thus the mother portion would be heaped onto the inheritance of the son receiving the birthrights. The eldest child is the primary recipient unless he swears it away, as in the case of Esau and Jacob. **Genesis 25:29-33 (KJV)** [29] And Jacob sod pottage: and Esau came from the field, and he *was* faint: [30] And Esau said to Jacob, Feed me, I pray thee, with that same red *pottage*; for I *am* faint: therefore was his name called Edom. [31] And Jacob said, "Sell me this day thy birthright." [32] And Esau said, "Behold, I *am* at the point to die: and what profit shall this birthright do to me?" [33] And Jacob said, "Swear to me this day;" and he sware unto him: and he sold his birthright unto Jacob. Once Esau Sware to exchange his birthright for food, the covenant was set and nothing could change it. However, Isaac is the father and could have overridden the commitment between the two boys and given the birthrights to Esau. However, Esau is made to Sware to the agreement, therefore it is binding and the birthright belonged to Jacob.

Esau is but one of a long list of people who lost their birthrights. Consider this, **1 Chronicles 5:1 (KJV)** [1] Now the sons of Reuben the firstborn of Israel, (for he *was* the firstborn; but, forasmuch as he defiled his father's bed, his birthright was given unto the sons of Joseph the son of Israel: and the genealogy is not to be reckoned after the birthright. Because Ruben defiled or had sex with one of his father's concubines, his birthrights were denied and given to Joseph. Now that we know how to receive a birthright and what the birthrights entail, consider this illustration. The father of three surviving children died leaving an inheritance is divided as such. The property is divided into four parts, the person receiving the birthrights would get one half (double portion) and the remaining children would get one forth each.

Firstborn Rights

Rights of the firstborn follow basically the same general criterion as do the birthrights. It is generally given to the elder son; however it is uniquely different from birthrights. In that the rights of the first borne includes special privileges and responsibilities. He was to act in his father stead, the leader of the family's possessions, all of His brothers and sisters would treat him as the father and priest of the family. Jesus was the firstborn to Mary and Joseph (Luke 2:7), and the older brother (Matthew 13:55 – 56) to James, Joses, Simon, Judas and sisters (unnamed) therefore, His natural position in life was to serve the family as head of household and priest. The priesthood automatically went to the elder son, with the exception of Ruben. Ruben, the older son of Jacob was excluded from the office of priest because of his adverse behavior toward his father. His rights as firstborn were given to Juda, and the rights of Priesthood given to Levi, and his birthright to the patriarch Joseph.

The firstborn appointment to the priesthood was a divine position, in that he was the person who acted on behalf to the family to God. **Hebrews 5:1-10 (KJV)** [1] For every high priest taken from among men is ordained for men in things *pertaining* to God, that he may offer both gifts and sacrifices for sins: [2] Who can have compassion on the ignorant, and on them that are out of the way; for that he himself also is compassed with infirmity. [3] By reason hereof he ought, as for the people, so also for himself, to offer for sins. [4] And no man taketh this honour unto himself, but he that is called of God, as *was* Aaron. [5] So also Christ glorified not himself to be made a high priest; but he that said unto him, Thou art my Son, today have I begotten thee. [6] As he saith also in another *place*, Thou *art* a priest for ever after the order of Melchisedec. Forever is never ending; this makes the covenant of Jesus a better covenant. Jesus is from eternity to eternity making his priesthood permanently established. Therefore, Jesus is able to keep you in the present of God always. He is not just High Priest forever because of His ability to live forever; but for these important reasons also: He was the perfect sacrifice, He is blameless and unspotted, He lived a life free from sin, and He does what the Law was unable to do. Jesus brought about salvation for the sins of man, whereas the Law only shows our weakness and need for salvation. The most important reason is because of Jesus' position as being equal with God and the Holy Spirit. He is truly the firstborn of God and elder brother of man.

Life before 30

As a child Jesus' family migrates from Israel to Egypt for security reasons. Later after the death of Herod, God call Him out of Egypt back to Israel, but somewhere along the journey

God diverts Joseph to Galilee. **Matthew 2:23 (KJV)** [23] And he came and dwelt in a city called Nazareth: that it might be fulfilled which was spoken by the prophets, He shall be called a Nazarene. At this point in the life of Jesus, the world concerning Him is silent. We do not here anything about His childhood and young adulthood. So what was Jesus doing? Jesus was 100% human and 100% God, but the time had not come for Jesus to take on His role as savior, therefore He lived as a human.

- Jesus learned and experienced all the everyday events and activities that affect the lives of humans.
- He learned how to provide for a family from Joseph, His earthly father.
- Joseph teaches Him the fine art of carpentry, and handing the business end of the family's estate.

Based on some of Jesus' teachings, I am sure that some of His customers purchased items, or labor using credit. And that not all of the customers paid their credit on time or even in full. Jesus had to learn how to deal with these and other social issues from the human perspective. Although Jesus was not subject to the same fundamental ends or human criteria; He was the firstborn of Mary and Joseph thereby making Him head of household after Joseph's death. Jesus was the person in charge; the responsibility of Mary and His other siblings rested squarely upon His shoulders until God called Him to the work of salvation. God calls Him as King of King and Lord of Lords. During this period, when the occasion arises for a king to visit one of his providences or inspect a city-state, someone from the providence or city-state is sent to clear the roads and welcome the arriving King. John the Baptist fills this role as the front runner for Jesus.

John The Baptist

Now that we have filled in the gaps as to what went on during the period of time that Jesus was waiting on the Father's instructions to execute his mission, it is time to explore Jesus' call to minister. Just because the Matthew's account of Jesus excludes thirty years does not mean that they were all silent, but it does show that Jesus waited on the Lord. Before Jesus comes on the scene, God sends a front runner, John the Baptist. John would continue to preach; repent yea for the Kingdom of Heaven is at hand. He used this phrase "Kingdom of Heaven," because he was a Jew and his message was to Jews. And because he was a Jew, talking to Jews he too held the name of God in awe. To the nation of Jewish people, the name of God was so precious and holy that they would not come out directly and say it. It was elevated above man's right to utter; therefore, in referring to God they used other descriptive terms. In this case, the Kingdom of God and the Kingdom of Heaven is one in the same place. John was the voice of the one crying in the wilderness. The word crying indicates a level of stress above the norm. John was crying out for people to repent and start following the Lord. More importantly, he was crying in the wilderness. The term wilderness is used in the Bible to show two opposite but equally portraits of life. As used in the Book of Numbers, God used the term wilderness to symbolize a fresh start for an oppressed people freed from the bondage of 400 years of slavery. However, Matthew's shows the other side of the coin; he paints the picture of a confused people slowly putting themselves back into bondage.

John the front runner is now denouncing that behavior, and disobedience to God. Who was this man John to denounce anything or want people to follow after him? John was the messenger from God, he saw evil and called it for what it was, and he was the 1st Prophet of Israel in 400 years. The people were glad to see him with exception of a few skeptics lurking in the background. These doubters hung on to John the Baptist's every word, judging in accordance with their politically correct models for religious worship, but John kept his eyes on God and called the nation to repentance. Offending people and being politically correct was not John's concern at this point. Because of his demeanor and raw freshness, his ministry summoned people from all walks of life. So who is this wild man called John the Baptist? He was the appointed of God to highlight evil and point people toward Jesus. His chief function was to clear the pathway for people to come to Jesus. Our Job in clearing the pathway for the unsaved to make the acquaintance with the only one whereby they may be spared that dreadful and terrible Day of Judgment has not changed. We must be a constant witness to the truth of Jesus Christ, and cry out boldly like John. John not only cried out in the wilderness, he wore strange clothing, as strange as those of Elijah. Both men dressed eccentrically and ate wired food (2 Kings 1:18). Elijah was the front runner of his time, and John would follow in his steps. We say that these men were front runner clearing the way, but what does this mean.

During the time of John the Baptist, the mindset of people caused them to fear three evils: *sickness* (because of poor medical practices and limited scientific knowledge about healing, people who became sick often died), *starvation* (famines in the land often brought about severe malnutrition which resulted in sickness and later death), and **travel** (of the three evils, travel was the worse. A person planning to travel was primed to do the following: write out last will and testament, assign the duties of firstborn and birthright to the elder son or person to take over the family, pay everyone owed money and return all borrowed items, provide for the family by telling them where the family treasure was buried, and saying good bye to everyone. When a person traveled, so much could go wrong, animal attacks while walking or sleeping, robbers wanting their goods, or just getting lost and perishing in the wilderness or desert). With the conditions of travel in mind, consider this, when Kings traveled, messengers would warn the cities to clear the way and make the way of the King straight. The cities-states in turn would sweep the streets and clear any debris or rubbish that may be in the path of the King. Jesus the King of Kings is traveling in your area, make the way straight and clear his path. Tell everyone about the good news of salvation. All of the obstacles that get in the way of a person's salvation must be swept aside. John is the first prophet in 400 years widely accepted as a man of God, who speaks the messages given to him by God. John is given the message of repentance, and he uttered it like a military drill sergeant in basic training. To achieve his objective, John cured these three intermediate objectives: the threat briefing, the promise, and the demands.

The Threat Briefing

The message of repentance was for everyone, however when he looked up and saw the Pharisees and Sadducees in attendance (Matt 7–12), all cameras focused on them. Like Jesus, John taught out of his experiences afar and from his surrounding communities. His messages addressed the historical and behavioral patterns of a corrupt group of peoples called the Pharisees and Sadducees. First, he wanted to know what they were doing at his baptism. Were they truly fleeing from the wrath to come like animals in the desert running from a brush fire, or just there to hinder others? John warned them not to depend on old glory saying (We have Abraham as our father). They must be upright and forthcoming for themselves because they would not be judged or get credit for the good deeds done by Abraham. John said "God is able of these stones to raise up seeds to Abraham," meaning that God does not just need a warm body to continue Abraham's seed. He could raise up stones in the support of Jesus. At the end of the threat briefing, John echoes the promise.

The Promise

A promise is something to look forward to; John gave them hope in the one who was to come. John made it clear that he was not the one that should come, but his job was to pave the way for the coming savior. Why is it necessary for John to run interference, educate, cure objections, and build an audience for Jesus? Consider this, when presidential or other political candidates are coming to your area, days or even weeks before they arrive, their party blasts the airwaves with information about the candidate. The candidate's platform and agenda are made public as well as the location of his/her visit. When the candidate arrives, there is no need to drum up a crowd, because the political party has already made his way straight in that area. Now all the candidate has to do is address the people. Well, in a sense, this is exactly what John does; he preaches that the Kingdom of God is at hand, meaning that the Kingdom of God is available for anyone, and people gather at his events awaiting this King. Keep in mind that John is a Jew, and preaches from the Jewish doctrine of the Spirit and not the Christian doctrine Holy Spirit. The difference is that the Jewish doctrine in this case is formatted in the spirit of the Greek influence of their culture. The thought process "doctrine of Spirit" brings about its root warrant in connection with the promise. The promise to man was satisfied in the beginning. In the beginning the Spirit blew breath into man and man became a living person. John's analogy then is this; the Spirit was breath, and breath is life, therefore we can receive that same promise to life again, because the promise of the Spirit is Life (Jesus) is available. After, preaching the Kingdom of Heaven is at hand, John does something more, he painted a vivid picture of Jesus and what will become of the unrighteous. **Matthew 3:10-12 (KJV)** [10] And now also the axe is laid unto the root of the trees: therefore every tree which bringeth not forth good fruit is hewn down, and cast into the fire. [11] I indeed baptize you with water unto repentance: but he that cometh after me is mightier than I, whose shoes I am not worthy to bear: he shall baptize you with the Holy Ghost, and *with* fire: [12] Whose fan *is* in his hand, and he will throughly purge his floor, and gather his wheat into the garner; but he will burn up the chaff with unquenchable fire.

CHAPTER 9

DARlsia Jacobs
49 YRS CANCER/lungs/liver
Husband unsaved Bro. Jacobs

John McCarthy
www.preceptustain.org
Galatian 3:1-29

Call to Commitment

—〰—

Just as John was committed to the mission God gave him of making the pathway straight. Jesus is just as committed to the Father's wishes that no man perish. In today's society our influences are stretched by an array of different inspirations. We are not to be taken in by every wind of doctrine, following everyone who seems to have all of the answers. When Satan attempted to sway Jesus in the wilderness, he offered Jesus all of the good reasons not to obey God, and follow him. Satan had all of the right answers, but his counsel did not line up with the Word of God. We as Christians are to do likewise, in both our lifestyle and walk with the Lord. Paul says in **1 Corinthians 9:24-27 (KJV)**

24 Know ye not that they which run in a race run all, but one receiveth the prize? So run, that ye may obtain. 25 And every man that striveth for the mastery is temperate in all things. Now they *do it* to obtain a corruptible crown; but we are incorruptible.

26 I therefore so run, not as uncertainly; so fight I, not as one that beateth the air: 27 But I keep under my body, and bring *it* into subjection: lest that by any means, when I have preached to others, I myself should be a castaway. Paul is saying here that when we look through the lens of the Scripture and examine ourselves by the Word, our picture should mirror a level of commitment to Jesus. Each person

has a different calling upon his/her life and that calling will determine the standards and conditions he/she must exemplify. The conditions are simple; Jesus has done all that is necessary for your salvation. He has paid in full the penalty of the Law, made it possible for you to walk in the spirit, set you free from the sting of sin and death, and given you liberty. Paul goes further to cause us to learn that like-kinds gravitate to its equal. In verse 5-8 he tells us that the thing of the flesh attend to the things of the flesh, and likewise the things of the spirit attends to the things of the spirit. Therefore, in our commitment to God as one of his pastors, elders, ministers, deacons, teachers or members, we must strive to identify ourselves with Christ instead of the flesh. Jesus is that perfect example of righteousness. When a person sees you in action, or deed, your goal should be to show them the love of God through Jesus Christ.

As stated previously, Jesus lived out the first 90% his life as the God-Man, fully God and Fully Man, doing the bidding of humanity. However, there comes a time when He must be about His Father's business. That last 10% of Jesus' life was dedicated to our salvation. For the last three years He walked the earth communicating to and teaching us how to obtain that perfect will of God. During that time Jesus' main objective was to teach the will of the Father. He shared information that pealed back the scales from our eyes for the first time and required an action. This action was sometimes implied, and sometimes a directive. Jesus' directives were so clear that ambiguity brought on by RELIGIOUS LEADERS such as the Pharisees or Sadducees could not prevent or confuse His message. His message was a clear call to action for people to change their ways and follow Him. In the military, after physical training, we would run between two to five miles. To make the run easy and show team spirit, we sang cadence, one of the cadences went something like this. One and two and three and four, (group repeat) run – run –

run and run some more (group repeat) pick up your weapon and follow me I am the airborne infantry. But Jesus called for humanity to follow him that it would result in more than just getting through the run. His call was to disciple teachable persons the way to salvation.

DISCIPLE

Jesus called to a group of rag tag unorganized group of Jewish boys, wanting to do nothing more than fish and have fun, was quite a change in their way of living. His work was cut out for Him in this highly diversified group of simple-minded people. Minister Hall, one of our pastors at the Life Center Church preached a series on unity, and one thing he said caught my attention is how much it cost to be a Christian. To belong to the body of Christ is not free, we have to give up our old ways of life and ascribe to the ways of the Master. Jesus' ministry began long before the disciples were called as followers, the Judges, Priests and Prophets were all committed. They pointed the way to Christ at great cost to themselves. Jesus knew that His disciples must be prepared for suffering. He Explained in **Matthew 10:24-25 (KJV)** [24] The disciple is not above *his* master, nor the servant above his lord.

[25] It is enough for the disciple that he be as his master, and the servant as his lord. If they have called the master of the house Beelzebub, how much more *shall they call* them of his household? Jesus it telling them to get ready because the same disrespect and confrontation that He faced from the world, they likewise will do so after His death. This passage asks His followers to sell out and give their lives to the cause of Christ at all cost, and they did. For example, Peter was hung upside down on a cross, and others with the exception of John met with fatal martyred cruel deaths. This teaching does more than just ask for blind obedience, it asks

for complete trust in God. Previously in Matthew Chapter 6, Jesus showed His disciples how God cared for everything and that their goal should be to seek God first and all other things would be added unto them. **Matthew 6:28 (KJV)** [28] And why take ye thought for raiment? Consider the lilies of the field, how they grow; they toil not, neither do they spin: [29] And yet I say unto you, That even Solomon in all his glory was not arrayed like one of these. God's saving grace reaches far beyond the flowers in the fields or the sparrow in her nest. Jesus was saying, Just trust God with your lives; but today with all the media outlets we as a people have learned to live highly guarded lives.

A guarded life is not what Jesus wanted. He wanted His followers to profess, preach the good news, and trust in God. Minister Young, the Life Center Church Outreach Leader has this little saying and before prayer or just talking at the mission while feeding the hungry; "Shout it from the mountain top" shout it out from the very present of your belief in God. Because we are Christians we profess God, and lift up His Name in Holy Adoration. If we cannot do that, Jesus says that we are in darkness and questions the degree of that darkness. Although we cannot gain salvation through our works, James says that our works is one of the tangible factors linking our faith to actions. The just shall live by faith and our faith in Christ must remain lucid or it will die. We must as minister Young says "Go tell it on the mountain top," but when we lunch out we must have a message. Our message of the good news must attend to the needs of the people.

COMMUNICATION

Communication is an interactive concept; it includes the activities of sharing information with other people. Communication is used also to convey ideas and teach others. Jesus was the communicator, teacher par excellence.

The table below provides a basic graphical illustration of Jesus' communication model

Communication Vehicle	Define	Method
Verbal	The process of sending and receiving messages with words, including writing and sign language.	Oral communication; speech.
Non-Verbal	sending and receiving messages without the use of verbal codes (words)	glance - eye contact (gaze) volume - vocal nuance gestures - facial expression (silence) - ..dress posture
Written	use of symbols	printed or handwritten)

In order for oral communication to be congruent the verbal or non-verbal, the body language must agree. If you are greeting a person saying something warm and friendly, but your body language says otherwise, the model is not congruent. Jesus was the great communicator, His body language always aligned with His Words. Jesus words were direct to the point and instruments of teaching the good news.

TEACHINGS OF JESUS

In Matthew 5:17 Jesus makes it clear that His intention is the fulfillment of the Law. In His Sermon on the Mount, Jesus taught His disciples against the religiosity that had taken root and weaved itself into the standards of godly living. The Old Testament Laws steaming from Moses and the Ten Commands and the Leviticus Laws on family living was far from the original intent. Laws governing wealth, family and civil violence, wealth and marital affairs was skewed to suite the values and benefits of the powerful. Jesus was offering through His controversial teaching a new way of interpreting the intent of these laws and their application to all people. Jesus taught love instead of getting even. **Matthew 5:38-39 (KJV)** [38] Ye have heard that it hath been said, An eye for an eye, and a tooth for a tooth: [39] But I say unto you, that ye resist not evil: but whosoever shall smite thee on thy right cheek, turn to him the other also. This is a powerful alternative to violence and an unheard of administration of peace. The Jewish community was not alone in their tendency to entertain violence. Our forefather also adhered to those concepts of violent activities and passed them along to us. We as the modern day Christians (not all) see the non violent teaching of Jesus as unrealistic. We think that it is necessary to physically defend ourselves and family at all cost. Consider this, one of the visiting pastors of my church (The Life Center Church) said that as a result of his daughter's kidnapping, he went ballistic. The mothers of the church, Minister and Deacons want him to pray about the matter. He told them to shut up and what to do with their prayers. This pastor temporally flipped, in his heart he wanted to avenge his daughter and punish the evil doer for that crime. These types of crimes are against one's self, In addition to violence, wealth and unfair treatment from the wealthy.

Mark 10:25 (KJV) [25] It is easier for a camel to go through the eye of a needle, than for a rich man to enter into the kingdom of God. Jesus warns about evil purpose and accumulation of wealth via ill gotten gains. Gains such as was attributed to the tax collectors in over charging people, you cannot serve God and money. And for marriage Jesus teaches that the intent of the heart is what exposes the person's sin. Whatever is within the person's heart defines the motive and intent? Jesus says that the adultery starts long before the actual activity. Matthew 5:28–30, **Matthew 5:28-30 (KJV)**

[28] But I say unto you, That whosoever looketh on a woman to lust after her hath committed adultery with her already in his heart.

[29] And if thy right eye offend thee, pluck it out, and cast *it* from thee: for it is profitable for thee that one of thy members should perish, and not *that* thy whole body should be cast into hell.

[30] And if thy right hand offend thee, cut it off, and cast *it* from thee: for it is profitable for thee that one of thy members should perish, and not *that* thy whole body should be cast into hell. But Jesus has compassion on people.

This week Bishop Kimble talked about compassion in quite a different way, and in some ways, his teaching like Jesus maybe hard to follow. As noted before, Jesus' teaching was new and radical or extremely to the right of homeostasis. On the surface Bishop Kimble could have ran for political office in any utopia on his platform of compassion and won. He talked about people less fortunate and fell victim to the economy. Compassion will not let you treat the poor, downtrodden and oppressed as an outcast. Bishop nailed it. Oppression of anyone is a serious injustice that is motivated and frosted by greed and callousness.

All of this gluttony and heartlessness has caused the economy of our compassion to collapse and consume us in the horror of terror and plunging hopelessness. If we follow Jesus in his examples and strong convictions for compassion, we will be more willing to forgive and live for the occasion.

The occasion is Jesus.

APPENDIX A

References

—⁓—

REFERENCE for the Occasion

Dr. Ronald F. Kimble, Bishop (formatting, leadership training) □ (DBS William Barclay, P1, 1975, 2nd ED) □ The Holy Bible KJV, Romans 6:3 – 12, Mark 16:15 – 18 □ Pastor William Abernathy □ Kesha M. Dawson □ Pastor Richard King

REFERENCE FOR CHAPTER 1, Abraham the Son of Promise.
Phase I Background Genesis 6 – 11

Every intent
Gen 8:21□Ps 14:1 – 3□Pr 6:18□ Mt 15:19, Ro 1:28 – 32□ Jer 18:7 – 10□ Grieved□ Isa 63:10□ Eph 4:30□
1. The flood (Gen 8:20 – 9:29) □
        Blot - Dt 28:63□Dt 29:20□
        Corrupt - Dt 31:29, Jdg 2:19
        Filled with violence - Eze 8:17□ I am sorry□ Gen 6:6□
        Am 7:3□ Am 7:6
An alter to - Gen 12:7 – 8□ Gen 13:18□ Gen 22:9
2. Noah's sacrifice to God and God's covenant with the Earth. (Gen 8:2 – 9: 19)
The fountain   Gen 7:11□ The rain Gen 7:4□ Gen 7:12□
Noah's sacrifice
        Clean animal Gen 7:2□ Lev 11:1 – 47□
        Burnt offering Gen 22:2, Ex 10:25

149

3. Noah Prophecy concerning the future of his children:
   a. Blessing
   b. Cursing
4. The Towel of Babel (Gen 10:1 – 11:26)

Phase II Abraham zeitgeist (Genesis 11:27 – 20:18)
- Family history
  o Mission to leave Ur (11:27 – 32)
  o Mission to leave Hebron)
- God's Covenant to Abraham (Gen 12:1 – 4 & 15: 1 – 5)

The promises in the covenant to Abraham were (1) Gen 12:1 Abraham is promise to be a great nation (land), (2) Gen 15:4 that his own son shall be his heir, and (3) Gen 12:2 he would be a blessing to all nations.

Counting the blessing one by one let's take a look at blessing number it is of abundance and increase (great nation and land).
  o Gen 15:4 that his own son shall be his heir,
  o (3) Gen 12:2 he would be a blessing to all nations.
- Terms and conditions of the covenant
- Heirs to the Covenant.

http://www.followtherabbi.com/Brix?pageID=1458
http://eword.gospelcom.net/comments/
http://www.biblegateway.com/resources/commentaries/
http://www.thefreedictionary.com/
These Were God's People, William C. Martin, M.A., B.D, 1966, p27

REFERENCE FOR CHAPTER 2, Deception
Bernice Johnson☐ Bishop Ronald F. Kimble ☐ Sophia J Dawson☐ Colossians 2:8 (KJV) note (KJV means King James Version, respectively) ☐ Matthew 12:35 (KJV) ☐ Genesis 3:1 – 4 (KJV)
Genesis 11 – ☐26. (KJV) ☐ Genesis 13 – 19 (KJV) ☐ Genesis 28 – 49 (KJV) ☐ Luke 17:28 -33 (KJV) ☐ 2 Peter 2:6 – 9 (KJV) ☐
How to Think Straight, Anthony Flew, 2002
http://www.friesian.com/relative.htm

http://www.bizjournals.com/houston/stories/2008/09/22/daily35.html"
as of October 9, 2008

Job 1 (KJV)

REFERENCE FOR CHAPTER 3, Unity
Ephesians 6:18 □ (KJV) James 4:2-3 □ (KJV) James 1:6-7 (KJV) □
Matthew 11:28 (KJV) □ Matthew 6:5 (KJV)□ Matthew 6:6 (KJV) □
Matthew 6:9-13 (KJV) □ (Dr. Randolph Bracy, Jr., Pastor (New Covenant
Baptist Church of Orlando)) □ John 14:13-14 (KJV) □ Romans 1:4-
5 (KJV) □ Ephesians 6:18 (KJV) □ Romans 10:17 (KJV) □ (Sophia
J. Dawson, my wife) □ Genesis 1:1-2 (KJV) □ Matthew 13:17(KJV)
□ Deuteronomy 29:29 (KJV) □ (Matthew Henry Concise) □ (Bishop
Ronald F. Kimble, Life Center Church, Eatonville FL) □ http://define.
com/URIM, http://define.com/THUMMIM. □ Exodus 28:30 (ASV) □
(1 Samuel 30:8 (ASV) □ 1 Samuel 28:6 (ASV) □ the Bible Answer
Man 1-888-ASK-HANK (275-4265)) □

REFERENCES FOR CHAPTER 4, DELIVERANCE
John 1:17 (KJV) □Leviticus 20:13 (KJV) □ Exodus 20:1-21□ (KJV)
Luke 24:44 □ (KJV) Romans 8:3-4 □ (KJV) **KJV** Matt 5:45 □ **(KJV**
John 3:16) □**KJV** Genesis 6:8 □ **(KJV)** Ephesians 2:5 □ **(KJV)**
Ephesians 2:8-10 □ **(KJV)** Galatians 5:4-6 □ John 6:48-51 □ (NASB95)
John 17:11 □ Isaiah 55:1 (KJV)

REFERENCE FOR CHAPTER 5, PRAYER
Acts 3:19 (GW) 1 Peter 5:7 (KJV) Ephesians 6:18 (KJV) James 4:2-
3 (KJV) James 1:6-7 (KJV) Matthew 6:5 (KJV) Matthew 6:6 (KJV)
Matthew 6:9-13 (KJV) (Dr. Randolph Bracy, Jr., Pastor (New Covenant
Baptist Church of Orlando)). John 14:13-14 (KJV) Romans 1:4-5 (KJV)
Ephesians 6:18 (KJV) Romans 10:17 (KJV) (Sophia J. Dawson, my
wife)

**REFERENCE FOR CHAPTER 6, GOD REVEALS HIS
MYSTERIES**
Genesis 1:1-2 (KJV) Matthew 13:17(KJV) Deuteronomy 29:29 (KJV)
(Matthew Henry Concise) (Bishop Ronald F. Kimble, Life Center
Church, Eatonville FL) (Sophia J. Dawson) http://define.com/URIM,
http://define.com/THUMMIM. Exodus 28:30 (ASV) question (1 Samuel
30:8 (ASV) (1 Samuel 30:81 Samuel 28:6 (ASV) the Bible Answer Man
1-888-ASK-HANK (275-4265)

REFERENCES FOR CHAPTER 7, FORGIVENESS
1 Corinthians 12:27-30 (KJV) (Ezekiel 18:18 – 29 http://prideandprej-
udice86.spaces.live.com/Blog/cns!37CF49520D7F9FF!130.entry. KJV
Heb 3:7 Romans 8:30 psalm 32 **Matthew 15:17-20 (KJV) Acts 16:25-**

31 (KJV) Isaiah 38:1-6 (KJV) Jonah 2:1-2 (KJV) Jonah 2:10 (KJV) Jonah 3:1-3 (KJV) Acts 9:10-18 (KJV) Genesis 2:16-17 (KJV) Genesis 3:22 (KJV) Matthew 10:16 (KJV) (KJV Matt 6: 14 – 15). (Matt 18:21 – 22) **Matthew 5:23-24 (KJV)**

REFERENCE FOR CHAPTER 8, JESUS OUR SALVATION
Ezra 2:60-63 (KJV) http://latter-rain.com/ltrain/herodg.htm **Genesis 1:26 (KJV) Matthew 22:42 (KJV) Isaiah 7:13-14 (KJV) Matthew 1:18-25 (KJV) Deuteronomy 22:23-24 (KJV) Numbers 5:11-30 (KJV) Isaiah 7:13-14 (KJV)** (Barclay, pp19). Isaiah chapter 7:1 – 14 (Isaiah 7:14) (Barclay, pp18 – 19) Genesis 1:26 – 28 Genesis 2:21 – 23 (Luke 1). **(Genesis 35:20 48:7) Micah 5:2 (KJV)** Matthew Chapter 2:1 – 12 Matthew 2:1-12 (KJV) **(Josh 19:15). (Gen 35:19), Micah 5:2 (KJV) Luke 2:4 – 7 (KJV)** (Acts 8:9 – 11) (Acts 13:6 – 8) **Matthew 2:13-18 (KJV)** http://en.wikipedia.org/wiki/Good_Thief#.22Dismas.3F.22 **Matthew 2:19-23 (KJV)** 1 Kings 12:12 (ESV) (Deuteronomy 21:17). **Genesis 25:29-33 (KJV) 1 Chronicles 5:1 (KJV)** (Luke 2:7), (Matthew 13:55 – 56) **Hebrews 5:1-10 (KJV) Matthew 2:23 (KJV)** (Matt 7 – 12)

REFERENCE FOR CHAPTER 9, CALL TO COMMITMENT
1 Corinthians 9:24-27 (KJV) Matthew 10:24-25 (KJV) Matthew 6:28 (KJV) Matthew 5:17 **Matthew 5:38-39 (KJV) Mark 10:25 (KJV) Matthew 5:28-30 (KJV)**

—⁊⁊⁊—

This book is straight forward and to the point. Michael has done a wonderful job in bringing to light God's Word to many of men's occasion. A must read for all Christian, young and mature.
BISHOP RONALD F. KIMBLE, D.D

Michael and his wife Sophia have five children and eleven grand children. The Dawson's are currently reside in beautiful Orlando Florida. He is a retired United States Army Vietnam Veteran and owner of Dawson Photography. Michael is a borne again Christian and an active member of the Life Center Church, Eatonville Florida. He currently serves in the outreach and education ministry. He spends several hours each day in private prayer, Bible study, and research. He is a verse by verse Sunday School Teacher, Bible Studies facilitator, and group discussion leader. He has earned a Master Degree in Business, has published several articles, and is the author of "The Wedding Planning Guide" currently in circulation. Michael believes in the trinity and accepts Jesus and Lord and Savior.

Printed in the United States
154585LV00002B/5/P

9 781607 918172